NUCLEAR WAR AND NUCLEAR PEACE

« NATO WATCH »
112, Rue Franklin
B - 1040 Brussels - Belgium

NUCLEAR WAR AND NUCLEAR PEACE

Gerald Segal
Edwina Moreton
Lawrence Freedman
John Baylis

First published 1983 by
THE MACMILLAN PRESS LTD
London and Basingstoke
Companies and representatives
throughout the world

Hardcover   ISBN 0 333 34087 6
Paperback   ISBN 0 333 34088 4

Printed in Great Britain by
THE PITMAN PRESS LTD
Bath

Contents

v

Introduction

Books about nuclear weapons have proliferated almost as fast as the weapons themselves, so why yet another book? We believe that the public debate is badly out of balance for, despite its quantity, much of the literature is dominated by a slanging match between extremist positions. This neither clarifies the problem for those properly concerned about the nuclear issue, nor offers realistic solutions.

We are not attempting to mark out a centre ground distinguished only by the fact that it is not extreme, nor do we wish to provide wishy-washy generalities. Our arguments and prescriptions are in some instances quite radical. Our distaste for the wishful thinking behind so many simplistic solutions runs deep, as does our desire to identify a coherent and positive set of policies that can offer some hope for the future. The analysis of nuclear war and nuclear peace is too complex an affair to fit into neat categories of right and left, of armers and disarmers. There are too many grey areas in the debate. But where the balance of judgement has to come down on one side or the other, we are not afraid of strange bedfellows.

We have all worked as British academics in related subjects and have written books and articles on various aspects of the issues. What we hope to do in this book is address the fundamental issues for a wider audience.

Our backgrounds are diverse: three are British and one is North American. We fall into the 'young' academic generation and have all been members of one protest group or another, from CND to anti-Vietnam war movements. We have also had opportunities to become fully acquainted with official thinking. Our work on these issues has not diminished our concern, but it has warned us off simplicities. Therefore the cover of this book has neither missiles, mushroom clouds nor doves of peace. That we feel strongly about the issues will be apparent when at times the style of this book becomes polemical.

Much of our argument inevitably is with the anti-nuclear movement for at the moment its voice is the loudest. We believe that this movement deserves to be taken seriously. This means neither dismissing it nor throwing pieties in its direction to prove that we too believe in peace. To take the anti-nuclear movement seriously is to engage in open and honest debate.

The four core chapters of the book are intended first to provide an introduction to the key problems in the nuclear weapons debate. Why do the weapons exist and is there really a Soviet threat that makes necessary the retention of the weapons? Second, we will argue that arms control is not dead and it offers our best hope for remaining neither 'red nor dead'. But arms control is neither a defence of the status quo, nor simple to achieve. Third, we will grasp the most prickly nettle of the current debate, and discuss the problem of nuclear weapons in Europe. What is the United States' strategy in the area, and how precarious is the peace? Finally, as a concession to our British base, and in recognition of the local nuclear weapons debate, we will examine the question of Britain's independent deterrent. Should Britain have nuclear weapons on its territory and, if so, should they be independent forces in addition to, or in place of, the American-controlled kind?

Joint authorship is always a delicate subject. The essential arguments in this book are ones that the four of us share. Hence the common introduction and conclusion. The four core chapters are written under individual names because there are variations in style and nuance which we have no desire to hide. But as a result of changes made after mutual criticism of first drafts, it is hoped that the book stands as a single coherent argument.

August 1982   Gerald Segal
                                                Edwina Moreton
                                               Lawrence Freedman
                                                  John Baylis

Glossary

ABM   Anti-ballistic missile. Designed to shoot down attacking missiles before they strike cities or other targets. So far they have not proven effective.

ALCM   Air-launched cruise missiles. Missiles which can fly at very low altitudes and can be programmed to follow the contours of the terrain to minimise radar detection.

ASBM   Air-to-surface ballistic missile. ICBMs launched from aircraft; also called air mobile missiles.

ASW   Anti-submarine warfare. Equipment designed to locate submarines and destroy them.

CND   Campaign for Nuclear Disarmament. British movement favouring unilateral nuclear disarmament.

END   European Nuclear Disarmament. Like CND but organised on a European (mostly West European) basis.

GLCM   Ground-launched cruise missile. Ground-based missiles. *See* ALCM

ICBM   Inter-continental ballistic missile. Ballistic missile with a range in excess of 5500 km.

INF   Intermediate nuclear forces. *See* LRTNF.

LRTNF   Long-range theatre nuclear forces. Nuclear weapons of a range between 1000 and 5500 km. They include such missiles as cruise, Pershing II and SS-20

MAD   Mutual assured destruction. Concept of reciprocal deterrence which rests on the ability of the nuclear weapons powers to inflict intolerable damage on one another after having survived a nuclear first strike.

MBFR   Mutual balanced force reduction. Subject of negotiations between NATO and the Warsaw Pact which began in Vienna in 1973.

MIRV   Multiple independently targetable re-entry vehicles. Re-entry vehicles carried by one missile which can be directed to separate targets.

NATO   North Atlantic Treaty Organisation. Western defence pact
           established in 1949.
SALT   Strategic Arms Limitation Talks. Negotiations between the
           United States and the Soviet Union initiated in 1969 which
           seek to limit the strategic nuclear forces of both sides.
SLBM   Sea-launched ballistic missiles. Ballistic missiles based on
           submarines and relatively invulnerable to an enemy first
           strike.
START   Strategic Arms Reduction Talks. Negotiations between
           the United States and the Soviet Union initiated in 1982
           which seek to reduce the number of nuclear forces of both
           sides.

1 Strategy and Survival

GERALD SEGAL

If politics is the art of the possible, then nuclear strategy is the art of the impossible. The word 'art' is appropriate because nuclear strategy is more concerned with the intangibles of politics, psychology, personality and perception. It is true that there is much science in nuclear weapons, in their design, development and deployment, but no strategy for their use could be subject to neat theories. Nuclear strategy is the art of the 'impossible' because in the final analysis nuclear weapons are too horrific for their use to be contemplated in a rational calculation of possibilities. Now that we are perched on this moral high ground, some might say that the discussion must end. Since you cannot use nuclear weapons, then it is a waste of time to discuss any strategy except the one of how to achieve rapid disarmament. Alas, the world of moral and intellectual purity is rarely the world of politics. Because nuclear weapons exist, and because there is an enemy against whom defence is perceived to be necessary, the art of nuclear strategy needs to be explored further.

It is important to point out that nuclear strategy does not have its origins in the clash between communists and capitalists. Indeed the first atomic bomb was developed for use against Nazi Germany and first used against Japan in the Second World War. This is important to keep in mind because some people see nuclear weapons as a cause of east–west conflict, rather than as a tool that, once invented, may become a part of international conflict.

The problem of nuclear weapons is often posed as merely a question of 'better red than dead'. This catch-phrase might lead some to believe that if we were all red, then the problem of nuclear weapons would go away. Hardly, because international conflict would continue and then some might wish to be 'better Chinese than dead' or 'better Nazi than dead'.

The problem of nuclear weapons is in fact a more complex, twofold

1

one. First, nuclear weapons have been invented and the genie, once escaped from the bottle of knowledge, cannot be replaced. Second, weapons are rarely the cause of conflict. It is political conflict that tends to determine the use of weapons, and continuing conflict in politics seems to be the natural process in international relations. The impossibility of un-inventing nuclear weapons cannot be overemphasised. Clearly the knowledge of how to make an atomic or hydrogen weapon is well known around the world, at least in theory. Even college students now grasp the essential principles. What is more, the expensive processing plants for nuclear technology are even more widely available, with lethal amounts of weapons-grade material produced and used in numerous power plants around the world. Those who would have us ban nuclear weapons by fiat, would have to wipe out nuclear knowledge as well as nuclear weapons stockpiles.

Not only is it impossible to suppress nuclear knowledge, but it is also crucial to understand that weapons are only dangerous because they are used as tools in political conflicts. In our own era of international relations, the most important international conflict is the one between communist and capitalist superpowers.

But if one accepts the inevitability of nuclear knowledge, there is no need to be fatalistic about the outbreak of nuclear conflict. Political conflict need not necessarily end in total war, nor must it necessarily use all the available weapons. Armed conflict can be avoided by deterrence, chance or change in the political process. Weapons may not be used if they are seen as ineffective, are superseded by other weapons, or all parties are deterred from using them. It is possible to stay neither red nor dead. We are therefore faced with the difficult problem of developing a strategy that allows us to live and yet defend our values.

This chapter will begin by tackling the question of morality in the discussion of nuclear strategy. It will then proceed to an analysis of whether there is a conflict of important values in contemporary international politics, and conclude by trying to make sense of the strategies for living in a nuclear world and how the dangers might be reduced.

THE MORAL HIGH GROUND

No one should be under any illusion that nuclear war is anything but horrific. But for some, the description of the effects of nuclear weapons is the end of the argument, and for others it is cause to skip the following paragraph with blasé mutterings of 'all war is hell'. Neither view will do, for if we are stuck in a world with nuclear knowledge, then the moral calculations must change. It is possible to be deeply concerned about the effects of nuclear war without abandoning all rational thought.

A typical nuclear weapon is one megaton (the equivalent to the explosion caused by one million tons of TNT – or fifty times the size of the Hiroshima bomb). If exploded at the optimum height it will destroy all brick houses in a $3\frac{1}{2}$ mile radius. The blast would hurl objects, including people or parts of skyscrapers, at lethal speeds to a $6\frac{1}{2}$ mile radius. Within that distance most fabrics will burst into flames. If exploded over Detroit it would kill half a million people outright and one million others would be wounded. Those unlucky enough to survive the heat and blast would be affected by radiation, even after the explosion. Unborn children subject to radiation would in all probability be born deformed. It should not take too much imagination to appreciate that even a few of these weapons, or the larger ones sitting atop modern missiles, would effectively eliminate social structures and life as we know it. It is not true that life would cease to exist, but the survivor's life might not be worth living in a 'republic of insects and grass'.

It is also true that nuclear destruction is not entirely unique in human experience. There have been gargantuan disasters, some of which have been man-made. One day's fire-bombing of Tokyo in the Second World War killed more people than did the Hiroshima atomic blast. The great plagues of 1348–50 wiped out more than a third of the population between India and Iceland. But these all pale in comparison to the destructiveness and the effectiveness of modern nuclear weapons. There can be no doubt that nuclear war, even on the most limited scale, cannot be seen as just another war.

But the discussion cannot end here. There are those who are so afraid of death that they will not make a will. Others will not take preventive action because they feel the odds are so steeply loaded against them. On the other hand, most people would feel it makes sense to plan in order to defer death.

Few aspects of any problem, including nuclear weapons, are clear cut or subject to simple solutions. Discussing the nuclear threat does pose moral dilemmas. It is at least as moral to try to do something to limit the threat of nuclear war. Moral purity is damaged if it allows violence to occur which might have been prevented by the exercise of a lesser amount of violence. Few would disagree with the view that nuclear weapons should, if possible, be eliminated. The question is how? Unfortunately there is no evidence that any weapon has been put back into the bottle of human ingenuity from which it escaped. Perhaps it could be done in a perfect world free of competing political systems, but there is not a shred of evidence to believe that mankind can unlearn a technology. Nuclear weapons are a good case in point.

It is certainly true that some weapons have been severely controlled by general international agreement, but they offer no hope to the unilateral disarmers. Dum-dum bullets were banned by mutual consent, but they were hardly decisive in war. Chemical weapons like nerve gas are prohibited from use (not manufacture and stockpile) and biological warfare (poisons of all sorts) is outlawed entirely. But these two types of weapons are not only difficult to use and above all to control in war, but more importantly they have been superseded in destructiveness by nuclear weapons. There is nothing like a new way of killing to make one forget about the previous evils. It may well be the case that if there were no nuclear weapons, we might be writing a book about chemical and biological war. As it is, the debate on the limits of these weapons is still continuing, although it is less in the limelight than nuclear weapons.

It is a central argument of this book that because one cannot unlearn technology and political conflicts are likely to continue, ways must be found of preventing the use of these weapons. It is not immoral to do so. Rather it is precisely because we appreciate the awesome power of these weapons that we feel so strongly about the need to think carefully about minimising their impact. This is not a path of inferior morality, but one of constructive morality. Although there are obvious differences, it is similar to the argument of those opposed to defeating the Nazi threat because it meant war and many deaths. But to do nothing to limit the Nazi evil because it meant some compromise with moral injunctions against death, was an abdication of responsibility.

There is another argument chipping away at the unilateralist's heights of morality. The retention of nuclear weapons is not merely for its own sake, but rather because they are also held by an opposing force. It is not possible to get very far in the nuclear weapons debate without coming up against this essential problem; must we consider the Soviet Union a threat? If the Soviet Union's values and social system are acceptable, then there is little problem. You don't see a

threat from Moscow and therefore there is little need to defend your-
self, possess nuclear weapons, or read this book.

To see the Soviet Union as a threat is to make a moral statement.
In a discussion of moral principles, it is important to make plain that
we face a moral dilemma. It is also crucial to remember that a consideration of the east–west conflict should involve a calculation of
whether one wishes to live in a society with values like those of the
Soviet Union. We would not argue that it is better to be dead than
red, but that there are other options. Given that nuclear weapons will
not go away (even if there were no communists and capitalists) and
the danger of nuclear war will remain, a central question is whether
east–west conflict is inevitable?

IS THERE A SOVIET THREAT?

If there were no international conflict, there would be no need for
nuclear (or conventional) weapons. If there is no enemy, then clearly
you need not be bothered by the fact that another state has some
coercive power that you lack. Unfortunately that kind of pacific
international environment does not seem to have existed in the past,
and does not appear to describe the present either. In the final
analysis, the necessity for retaining nuclear weapons derives from the
existence of a similarly armed enemy. The weapons follow rather
than precede the original conflict. It is also important to suggest that,
had nuclear weapons existed in other non-east–west conflicts, for
example in the Second World War (for which they were invented) or
even earlier European conflicts, the dangers of nuclear war would
probably have been similar. So long as there is an enemy with impressive power, it is surely supreme folly not to have countervailing
power. Even if the threat is not certain, it is only prudent to retain
some way of responding to potential threats.

Thus it is central to ascertain whether the Soviet Union is a threat.
Proof in such matters of assessing threat is notoriously difficult: the
only real proof may come after the threat has materialised and when
it may be too late. Both extremes of the nuclear weapons debate
shout loudly that they know the Soviet Union to be either a dangerous imperial power or a defensive peaceful power. No one can be
sure. In trying to answer the question, two main areas of evidence can

be suggested; what are the capabilities and what are the intentions of the Soviet Union?

SOVIET CAPABILITIES

Let us take the capabilities of Soviet power first and compare them to those of the west. Different numbers are bandied about depending on which side of the argument you wish to support. It is not so much that analysts use different numbers for the same type of weapons, but more that they attempt to compare different types of weapons, some of which are held in greater numbers by one side. So if we begin with basics – how much money do the US and Soviet Union spend on their armed forces – the problems in counting become immediately apparent. It is clear that the Soviets spend roughly twice as much of their GNP on military items as the US. It is true that the Soviet GNP is lower than that of the US, but even in absolute terms the Soviets seem to spend more. Unfortunately the argument cannot end here, because such calculations assume that the Soviets obtain as much 'bang for the buck' (or rubble for the ruble) as does the US. But clearly such costing is vague and uncertain, if only because it is generally accepted that the Soviet economy is not nearly as efficient as that in the west. So the Kremlin probably gets far less for the greater sums it spends. What is more, if similar figures are compared for the entire Warsaw Pact and NATO alliances, the west spends roughly the same as the eastern bloc despite using up a smaller percentage of their much more powerful GNPs. Perhaps the only clear conclusion to emerge from these confusing figures is that while there is no real Soviet superiority, but rather a rough parity, it is also clear that Soviet spending on the military is impressive. To offer no defence against such power, if it is deemed to be a threat, would be unwise and dangerous.

What about actual Soviet forces? Are they designed for offence or defence? By the early 1980s the Soviet Union clearly had more strategic delivery vehicles (missile launchers and bombers) than the US. Most assessments credit the Soviet Union with a 25 per cent lead in inter-continental ballistic missiles (ICBM) and sea-launched ballistic missiles (SLBM), with the US having a 2–1 lead in the much smaller category of heavy bombers. The overall Soviet advantage in all categories is about 15 per cent.

Missile and bomber numbers meant much more when only one

warhead could be placed on each rocket, but now, in the era of multiple independently targetable re-entry vehicles (MIRVs), it becomes more important to count the total of warheads, not missiles or launchers. In this category the US held a 30 per cent advantage in 1980 but with Soviet MIRVing of its own missiles, the gap is rapidly narrowing. The Soviet Union's missiles are also 'heavier', i.e. they can carry more warheads than their US counterparts so, if fully MIRVed, would give Moscow an even greater advantage. However, as US missiles are marginally more accurate, they can be expected to achieve their assigned task more effectively and therefore require fewer warheads. In addition, much of the US force is on faster reaction standby than its Soviet equivalents, with more SLBMs on station and bombers on alert. In sum, it is difficult to suggest with any certainty that the Soviet Union or the US has any 'lead' in strategic nuclear weapons. Once again, rough parity seems to be the best way of describing the state of the east–west balance.

The balance of power in Europe is an even more complex problem and will be discussed in Chapter 3 in greater detail. But it is important to point out here that the overall conclusion of slight Soviet advantage in a generally balanced confrontation is the same as on the strategic level.

Several important mitigating factors are often cited in explanation of the massive Soviet power. First, many people acknowledge that there is a Soviet tendency, derived in part from traditional approaches to defence and perceptions of threats from the west, to overinsure. They try to compensate for western advantages in technology and innovation with greater numbers of their own. Tradition also helps to explain an excessive Soviet fear of invasion and the devastation caused by wars (past attacks came mostly from the west).

Second, there is the problem of a strong military institution in the Soviet Union that insists on higher spending so as to protect its bureaucratic position. In the closed Soviet society the military controls information about defence issues and therefore can argue powerfully for more military spending. Third, the Soviets are said to be more deeply concerned than the west about the reliability of their allies. Especially in Europe, a great deal of Soviet power is said to be needed to hold on to Eastern Europe as much as to threaten the west. It is paradoxical that the Soviet Union is the only power surrounded by hostile communist states.

The Soviet Union's capability is clearly impressive and roughly equal to that of the US. If the Soviet Union had no intention of threatening anyone, then that balance of power is a waste of money and dangerous. On the other hand, the balance is comforting if the Kremlin intends to attack or pressure. The Soviet capability in itself does not prove anything, beyond the fact that if it so desired, and there were no opposition, the Soviet Union has the power to coerce in a particularly horrific way. The most important question is what are Soviet intentions?

SOVIET INTENTIONS

Some would argue that the Soviet Union has merely inherited the Tsarist dreams of imperial glory. Thus expansion is in the soul of the Kremlin leadership and, given half a chance, the hordes will come pouring across the central European plains. This extreme scenario cannot be proven right or wrong. It is perhaps more useful first to approach Soviet intentions from what they say they want to do rather than what some in the west fear they may want to do. The ideology of any communist state, and preeminently the state that pronounces itself leader of the communist world, is an important source of evidence. It is not a question of the west saying the Soviet Union has an expansionist ideology: the Soviets say so themselves. The concept of inevitable change of international society in the direction of communism is not a figment of the paranoid's imagination, it is clearly elucidated Soviet policy. The Soviet Union is not a status quo power in its declaratory policy. One may question whether its leaders mean what they say and whether they will achieve their objectives in dangerous and violent ways (and we will do so below). However, the ideology of revolution exists. When the former Soviet leader Nikita Khrushchev said 'we will bury you', he may not have meant in nuclear rubble, but he did believe that his side would win in the end.

This is crucial to an understanding of how the Soviet Union views its own foreign policy. It is often misleadingly thought that the Soviet Union accepts the notion of peaceful coexistence in the same sense of maintaining the status quo as conceived in the west. There can be little question that this ethnocentric view fundamentally misunderstands the revolutionary purpose of the Soviet state. Rather than peaceful coexistence, the Soviet Union subscribes to the idea of competitive coexistence. Coexistence, because nuclear war is too horrific. But also competition where it is less dangerous to pursue it, because the two ideologies of communism and capitalism are fundamentally irreconcilable, at least in the long term. The struggle between two forces – or the correlation of forces – is not merely a military calculation, but it does suggest that some kind of conflict is inevitable. So while the prophets of doom on the right argue that the Soviet Union is uncontrollably dangerous they make one type of error, the prophets of peace on the left miss the continuing nature of ideological struggle.

For some, the image of a communist world is not bad because, according to their own values, a mixed economy is unacceptable. Those who do not see communism as a threat, need not see the Soviet Union as a threat, although some renegade European or Asian Communist Parties might disagree. These communists might in fact be more concerned with Moscow's imperial pretensions rather than its ideology. But in the west it is necessary to stress the centrality of differing systems of values underpinning the ideological conflict. There should be little confusion over the fact that some of the most basic freedoms that westerners take for granted are not tolerated in the Soviet Union. Many people may carp about our biased press, Official Secrets Act, police brutality, restrictive trade union legislation or passive Parliament, but they are not a patch on the restrictions in the Soviet Union. The Berlin wall or rigid emigration laws in the Soviet Union are intended to keep citizens inside, not to prevent westerners from flooding in. You may choose the limited benefits of the Soviet system, for example in providing the 'right to work', but it is important to assess the significance of your right to choose systems. There are real differences between east and west, and if western values can be defended without undue risk, then it is worth doing.

Some argue that the Soviet Union holds to its revolutionary values but does not seek to impose them upon others, or if it does, then it will avoid undue risk in the process. There is much to commend this line of argument, but it does not question the existence of real differences between east and west. The first part of that argument sees no active Soviet threat, while the second sees the need for countervailing power. What has been the past evidence for these different views and how active has the Soviet threat been?

Since the Russian Revolution in 1917 the Soviet Union has expanded its territory to include the Baltic states; after the Second World War, it took some territory from Poland, Japan and China. Of those lands, only the Chinese territory was returned, and then to an allied communist state. Direct Soviet spheres of influence have expanded since 1945 to include the East European states and, in the

1970s, Afghanistan to the south. Apart from the Chinese case, the only territories occupied by Soviet troops and then given back independence include Korea, part of Austria and northern Iran. If there is a pattern in all this, it is expansion, but cautious in its means.

In the nuclear realm, the Soviet Union has issued few explicit threats, and unlike the US has not used atomic weapons. Khrushchev's threat against Britain and France in the 1956 Suez Crisis and against China in the 1969 border dispute, are the only explicit cases of Soviet brinkmanship in the nuclear field. The US can be accused of similar action against China, in Korea, in the Middle East and preeminently in the Cuban missile crisis of 1962. Once again the Soviet Union is not inclined to take great risks in the use of its military power, but even in the nuclear realm, threats have been made. Without a countervailing power, the outcomes may well have been different. But what does this say about Soviet intentions?

The Soviet Union seems to use military force to assist the revolutionary process, but it does so carefully with a conservative calculation of risks. The level of risk and likelihood of the use of force tend to rise the closer one approaches what the Soviet Union has deemed to be its core security area. Thus, at its most immediate ring of security, the Kremlin would hardly pause to secure its defence, for example by seizing the Baltic states or retaining Japanese islands. Then there is the crucial East European buffer which since the cold war era has seen no major change. Unrest and unorthodoxy in East Germany, Poland, Hungary and Czechoslovakia were all met with varying degrees of force to keep those countries in the Soviet sphere. More diversity in the bloc was tolerated in the southern tier where Romania, and especially Albania and Yugoslavia, were allowed to slip out of firm control, although none have approached anything like a pro-western let alone a genuinely neutral position.

Other crucial territory along the Soviet border has been subject to Soviet pressure and in some cases the use of force. China was too large and powerful to be subjected to the same kind of coercion applied to Afghanistan in 1979. Northern Iran was returned to independence after strong western threats. What is clear is that without a strong outside force, the Soviet Union seems to feel it has greater freedom to determine the political future of its neighbours. In some cases the risks taken are higher, but in all cases there is an explicit calculation as to the strength and resolve of the local power or its western supporters. The Soviet Union may argue that it is acting for defensive reasons when it intervenes in the affairs of neighbouring states, but in most cases it is a question of the local state seeking greater independence and the Kremlin imposing control if it can. Even without an opposing western power, this Soviet expansion for 'defensive' reasons would be likely to continue because the local states are likely to continue to desire independence.

Other neighbours of the Soviet Union have had more independence for a number of historical and political reasons, but they all are at least implicitly dependent on the presence of western power to secure their neutralism. Finland is said to have been neutralised in a pro-Soviet tilt (hence 'Finlandised', meaning a somewhat pro-Soviet regime) but the extent of its independence appears to depend on a combination of the state's own history and the proximity of NATO power. Neutral Austria is less 'Finlandised' but this is largely because of western power in the early days of the cold war and the west's insistence on an independent Austria. Similarly Sweden's independence seems to rest on its own history of independence and a clear perception on both sides of the Iron Curtain that Sweden should remain independent.

Yet another category of states are those bordering on Soviet security zones and subject to more subtle Soviet pressure to adjust their policy. West Germany is a special case. Because it lies on the other side of the cold war line, Bonn's leaders tend to bend rather more when Moscow breathes hard. Other border states like Pakistan react in a similar manner and also depend on explicit US guarantees for their independence.

This pattern of Soviet pressure and western counterpressure over the bodies of independently-minded states is less crucial further away from Soviet security spheres. Events in the Middle East, Africa or Southeast Asia indicate that Moscow surely seeks influence and exerts pressures where it can. But the Kremlin takes fewer risks in areas of less importance. In these cases, countervailing western power is often of less importance to the outcome than is the fierce independence of the local states. Soviet power also extends far less effectively at those distances.

Thus there is no simple answer to the question whether there is a Soviet threat. The threat does seem more visible the closer one comes to what Moscow deems its security sphere. Whether for defensive motives or not, the Soviet Union is at its most threatening when dealing with independently-inclined neighbours. At some undefined line of containment, the countervailing power of western states makes it clear to the Soviet Union that the independence of these states must be maintained.

The risks to the Soviet Union are raised and Moscow lowers its pressure. To remove the counterpressure would permit Soviet expansion.

This is not to cry 'the Russians are coming, the Russians are coming'. They are unlikely to come on tanks if they do, for more subtle pressure would be preferred. Western Europe remains a target of Soviet political pressure. It would be folly to presume that because the Soviet Union has not yet been successful in changing the post-Second World War lines in any major way, that it does not seek to do so if it could at low cost. Europe is the region where the link between military and political security is strongest, but where that link could be seriously undermined. It is clear from a Soviet point of view that while there can be a military stalemate between east and west, there is no such thing as neutrality in political and economic terms. Faced with a neutral, disarmed Western Europe, the Soviet Union would probably not want to occupy it. But it would certainly wish to control it politically and economically. If Europeans want to defend their own democracies they have to be ready to defend themselves. It has been an oft-repeated political truism that one-sided impotence does not prevent aggression by a stronger state. Unilateral disarmament would at the very least swap one kind of military insecurity for another. Nuclear weapons, as long as they remain part of the military balance, compel east and west to coexist. Their political differences compel them to be able to deter each other.

Some suggest that the Soviet Union is so jumpy about events close to its borders merely because it feels threatened and vulnerable. Remove the countervailing power and the Soviet Union would relax. The evidence provides little ground for such optimism. One need only reflect on the extent to which the Soviet Union rejects any substantive diversity in its own sphere of influence, to see the less than benign Soviet intentions. Moscow's unwillingness to tolerate much diversity within its own bloc is as clear an indication as any of Soviet intentions towards Western Europe. There is no way to be sure that the Soviet Union would not exert pressure on its neighbours and the risk of finding out is not worth the potentially permanent loss of independence. At a very basic level, national independence rests on a will and an ability to defend oneself. The central problem remains: how to offer resistance to a Soviet threat, without unduly risking war. There are both relative threats and relative risks in the threat of nuclear war. Relativity supposes policy options. These are grey areas of politics rather than the simplified black or white of extremists. We now turn to an explanation of the shades of grey of nuclear weapons strategy in order to ascertain whether reasonable resistance can be offered with reasonable risks, to what we have seen to be at least the likelihood of a Soviet threat.

DETERRING THE ADVERSARY

The doctrine designed to offer reasonable resistance with reasonable risks is called deterrence. Deterrence is basically the attempt by one side to make its adversary refrain from taking certain actions by openly threatening to make such action too costly. This doctrine is more complex in practice, but this basic desire to prevent unwanted action by threat lies at its core. It is not a new idea and has operated as long as there has been conflict between men or states. Deterrence only now comes under such severe scrutiny because it is being called upon to prevent a nuclear war, and if it fails, the implications are too horrific to contemplate.

Deterrence has undergone many changes and has been the subject of myriad debates among those concerned with nuclear strategy precisely because it is being asked to do so much. There are serious problems with nuclear deterrence, but so far it seems to have been crucial in preventing a nuclear war. At first, the US as the sole possessor of atomic weapons did not think very seriously about the implications of its new power. For many, the weapon was seen as deterring a Soviet conventional attack in Europe and as such would allow the US to maintain smaller conventional forces. At that time the US merely threatened to deliver a bomb on Soviet cities if the Soviets used their conventional power against western targets. Neither the theory nor the threat were very sophisticated. With the loss of the American monopoly of atomic weapons in 1949 and the rapid move to more powerul nuclear weapons, it became clear that in considering war in the nuclear age the US faced a revolution in military thinking. In 1954 the US responded with a crude deterrence doctrine labelled 'massive retaliation'. Briefly stated, it was American policy to respond with massive attacks on Soviet cities if the Soviet Union launched any sort of attack around the world. Massive retaliation had the advantage of being cheap, for the relatively inexpensive nuclear weapons were seen to eliminate the need for a massive conventional build-up that could cope with growing Soviet power. This problem of nuclear weapons as an inexpensive deterrent, and its potential higher risk, has remained a feature of much criticism of nuclear weapons. How much should one pay for a safer defence? The decline of massive retaliation strategy had nothing to do with cost, and more to do with the obvious (even at the time) argument that it was not a credible deterrent. Since deterrence had never been tested and a nuclear war never fought, much nuclear strategy turns on this crucial question of whether the deterrent is credible. It was appreciated that it was incredible for the US to threaten a massive nuclear retaliation on Soviet cities if Moscow was, for example, restricting traffic to West Berlin or supporting revolutionary war in Vietnam. Deterrence had to be more than a black and white surrender or suicide proposition. Some deterrents were better than others, and hence safer.

The search for greater credibility encouraged the idea of developing a more flexible response to differing kinds of threats. By the early 1960's the US felt it could make its deterrence more credible if it could not only threaten to attack Soviet cities known as counter-value targets (as if everything else was not valuable), but also attack Soviet military sites (known as counterforce). According to the theory, there were now more flexible responses to more limited threats of war and so an attack could be more credibly deterred. It seems sensible, but was it?

Theorists were quick to point out problems in the notion of flexible response. If there were flexible options, with smaller weapons, then the threshold of nuclear war was lowered. When war was too horrific to contemplate because it would wipe out millions of people, surely war was less likely to be started. Once it did, it would be totally devastating. Victory for either side would be meaningless. Now that it was possible to conceive of limited war, then some might feel they could fight that kind of war and still talk of victory as a meaningful outcome. Paradoxically, the doctrine of flexible response attempted to control nuclear war in a way that massive retaliation could not, but many believed that it made such a war more likely, if less devastating.

Throughout the 1960s the US established their nuclear forces without fully resolving the doctrinal difficulties. Most strategists seemed to accept that there were problems with any doctrine of deterrence, but there was no choice but to try to make it work. Living with the grey areas of strategy was not comfortable, but then the entire question of nuclear strategy and the Soviet threat was a grey area. The dominant doctrine of the 1960s for US strategy was something called 'assured destruction', i.e. that credibility of deterrence would be ensured if the US could maintain a clear and unmistakable ability to inflict unacceptable damage upon the Soviet Union – even after absorbing a surprise first strike. Unacceptable destruction was defined as killing one fifth to one third of the Soviet population and destroying one half to two thirds of its industry. If this assured destruction were mutual, as many had come to accept as inevitable, then nuclear strategy could be seen to be based on mutual assured destruction (MAD).

In order to ensure deterrence, what the US needed was both flexible options and the security that its nuclear forces could survive a surprise attack. These two strands of deterrence did not always produce the same kind of forces, as counterforce strategy suggested the need for more accurate weapons, while at the same time the new accuracy undermined assured destruction by threatening a possible first strike. But for the meantime, these subtleties were not appreciated as strategic policy was made on the 'shifting sands' of political compromise and not always according to simple rationality. The search for survivability of forces in case the enemy struck first meant that assured destruction sought an invulnerable second strike weapon. So long as there were weapons that could survive and still threaten to retaliate with assured destruction, credible deterrence would be maintained.

This was in part the rationale behind the evolution of the American triad of nuclear forces. The idea was that even if one leg of the triad of nuclear forces, e.g. land-based missiles, was attacked (25 per cent of US forces), there would still be two other legs, bombers (25 per cent of forces) and submarines (50 per cent of forces), which could retaliate. In order to enhance the chance of surviving, missiles were put in hardened silos so as to ride out a first strike, bombers were kept on alert or in the sky where they were less vulnerable, and above all missiles were placed on submarines and sent into the deep blue sea to hide from the potential Soviet first strike. It takes little imagination to see that although the motive for these developments was defensive, it complicated any attempt to limit nuclear weapons. What is more, it became harder to find a clear point at which one could say how much was enough to carry out these tasks. The problem was preeminently one of psychology and politics, and only then a technological one.

The absurdity of constantly building more forces was not only evident to nuclear disarmers. The problem was to define what was sufficient for deterrence. For this, and other reasons, the process of pursuing arms control agreements began in earnest in the late 1960s (see Chapter 2) and the US began to speak of a doctrine of sufficiency. This doctrine was not opposed to deterrence or MAD, but rather represented an attempt to define at what point there could be confidence of having achieved deterrence. Nothing much had changed in nuclear strategy, but people were now earnestly trying to limit the amount of nuclear force. It was an admirable attempt, for it accepted that there was no escape from the grey areas.

Despite much carping from some critics on the left and right, not much has changed in US strategic thought. Throughout the 1970s the Americans drifted into a more explicit definition of flexible response. The new doctrine of 'limited strategic options' meant little more than sharpening up the ability to strike at specific targets that were not cities. In the 1960s these options were understood more in terms of theory and few were targeted in practice, largely because the technology was not available. When it became possible to target the 'side of a barn door', or at least land within 300 feet of a target, the era of limited strategic options had truly arrived.

Although warheads are now more accurate, the problems with such flexible options are still no different. Under such conditions a nuclear war became more thinkable and because theoretically it could be more limited, it could also be a more useful instrument of policy. The theory remained the same: it was more credible to deter a limited strike with an equally limited strike. It also made more sense to limit a nuclear war if possible. Attention then began to focus on how to keep such a war limited and many strategists pointed out that even limited nuclear attacks would cause serious disruption to communication and control. By the early 1980s a great deal of money was being spent in the US on precisely this problem; how to keep a nuclear war limited. There was now a new round of military spending that was driven by one defensive reason, but having other, more offensive and dangerous implications. Ensuring credibility meant having limited strategic options, but these more accurate options could also be seen as threatening a destabilising first strike or making the option of nuclear war more thinkable. There was a clear need to develop a mix of weapons that ensured deterrence, and in the least dangerous way.

But finding such a mix of weapons has never been easy. Some critics denounced MAD when it was the ruling US nuclear doctrine, but when MAD was refined to cope with the critics' comments, many became even more upset. Now they saw limited strategic options as even more dangerous and blamed the US government for the change. The criticisms might well have been better aimed at the other super-power, for although they reject the notion of limited nuclear war as a practical possibility, in practice it was the Soviet Union that first conceived of nuclear weapons as part of a war-fighting doctrine. No assessment of how to find the least dangerous mix of weapons for deterrence can really be carried out without reference to Soviet strategic thinking.

SOVIET STRATEGIC THINKING

Nuclear strategy, and the problems in dealing with grey areas of credibility, are not confined to US strategists. It would have been convenient if both the Soviet Union and the US had come up with the same 'solutions' to strategic problems, but they did not. Thus deterr-ence is less secure, credibility more uncertain, and military spending largely unchecked.

The American doctrine of assured destruction is based on the assumption that deterrence is achieved by threatening unacceptable punishment to the other side. For numerous reasons, the Soviet Union seems to argue that deterrence should be based on denying the enemy any reasonable hope of victory. Thus deterrence by denial is to be achieved by demonstrating the ability to fight a war on any level without losing. But such a 'war-fighting' doctrine has the unfor-tunate requirement of nearly unlimited means to satisfy Soviet defence planners' paranoia. Because of an ideology that distrusts the west; because of a military that does not wish to leave defence depen-dent on the assured destruction of the enemy; and because of a history that makes the Soviet Union wary of vulnerability to attack, Moscow rejects US deterrence doctrines. Thus a key premise of US strategic thought, that deterrence would be based on mutual assured destruction, is not valid.

This is not merely an esoteric difference of strategy, for as we have seen in nuclear thinking, strategy has important implications for the development of powerful weapons. Unlike the US, which emphasised weapons of assured destruction and only recently weapons for limited strategic options, the Soviet Union has a more complex war-fighting doctrine. Deterrence by denial argues for a wide range of forces to ride out an attack (civil defence), to limit the damage (air defence) and to wage war in return (missiles and bombers). The US's assured destruction sees no point in the first two tiers as defence is impossible. Since the US seems unable to persuade the Soviets of this MAD argument, then there is one-sided rather than mutual assured destruction. What is worse, the presence of the first two tiers in Soviet doctrine only encourages the US to develop more sophisticated and accurate technology so as to penetrate Soviet defences and assure destruction. Arms spending grows as a result.

Furthermore, a greater proportion of Soviet strategic nuclear forces are of the most dangerous type of weapon. Seventy-five per cent of Soviet strategic weapons are land based (compared to 25 per cent in the US) and because they are in fixed silos, they are more vulnerable to being hit in a preemptive attack. They also have the most accurate warheads and so are more able to threaten a first strike against the US. This is not to say that Soviet strategic forces are designed for offensive purposes. Problems of geography that limit Soviet naval power, problems of history that give a bias to land forces, and problems of inter-service rivalry that give preeminence to certain types of heavy, offensive missiles, all contribute to create what looks like an offensive posture from defensive motives.

Once again, both sides proceed from essentially defensive motives, but neither is convinced of the other side's good intentions. With differing strategic doctrines the arms control process becomes more complicated, but not impossible (see Chapter 2). Both sides share some crucial strategic precepts even if they disagree on others. Both believe in the need for deterrence and defence, although they attain these elusive objectives in different ways. Both sides also believe that nuclear war, other than the most limited sort, is so destructive as not to serve as a useful instrument of policy. Khrushchev said that the 'atom bomb does not obey the class principle' and it will kill capitalists as easily as communists. But both sides conceive of, and plan to deter, limited nuclear war. For the Soviet Union this is part of deterring by denial, i.e. that war can be fought at any level. For the US, limited strategic options enhance the ability to punish at any level of threat. The doctrines may differ, but the fact that they also agree on many crucial topics suggests that it might be possible to reach a mutually acceptable arms accord.

Because of these complexities, reaching an arms control agreement cannot be simple. Because in the final analysis the negotiators are dealing with human psychology, mutual insecurities and the undefinable limits of credibility, there is a need to move carefully towards arms limitation with mutually reinforcing steps. Simply pointing to the amount of overkill possessed by the superpowers is not reason enough for either one of them to reduce numbers of weapons. There exist logical explanations for the vast proliferation of weapons, and the nuclear knot must be untied with recognition of the intricacies that went into the original weaving.

DOES DETERRENCE WORK?

It can hardly be denied that the analysis of nuclear weapons issues has become very complex, but in many respects it has become too sophisticated for its own good. As with many previous military scenarios, it may be 'magnificent', but it is not strategy. We tend to lose sight of the need to keep deterrence as the centrepiece. Much of the discussion of convoluted doctrine, sources of policy or institutional rivalries obscures the need to appreciate that deterrence of a potentially threatening Soviet Union armed with nuclear weapons is at the heart of the present nuclear strategy. This is essentially achieved by maintaining forces for credible assured destruction.

So far deterrence, in all its variations, seems to have worked at keeping the peace between the nuclear powers. Reasonable resistance to the Soviet threat has been offered by running reasonable risks. So far, the calculation of risk has been understood by both sides. One cannot prove that it is deterrence that has done the trick, but deterrence certainly has not failed. This is another grey area. It also cannot be proven that deterrence will continue to work, but it seems reasonable to continue operating in this grey area until a better solution can be found. Some people don't like living with such uncertainty and this is an understandable sentiment. It would be comforting if the uncertainty could be eliminated, but since uncertainty seems to have been the norm in previous military history, it may be unreasonable to expect anything more of the present or future. Chemical and biological weapons have existed for some time, but by and large deterrence seems to have prevented their use. In smaller-scale conventional wars, for example between the Arabs and Israelis in 1967 and 1973, there has been effective mutual deterrence not to attack each other's cities. Of course deterrence can both succeed and fail. In the Second World War both sides attacked civilian populations but neither used poison gas. What is more important is that it *can* also work and keep a kind of peace. The Second World War example is not proof, but it is strong evidence that deterrence may be a way of coping with the grey area.

Some would suggest that even if deterrence works, it is unaccept-able because it is immoral. For war to be moral it must obey the two basic precepts of a just war: keep the level of force proportional to the intended aim and discriminate between combatants and non-combatants. In theory a limited war that was confined to military targets would not violate either of these principles and thus could be called moral.

Nuclear strategy that seeks to deter by threatening to destroy cities would seem to violate both principles. However, it can be argued that the threat to inflict damage is not morally unacceptable if it is not carried out. What is important is the consequence of the action, and if deterrence keeps the peace where absence of deterrence does not, then deterrence is moral. Of course it is possible that deterrence will fail. Then the act of carrying out the threat to destroy cities could be considered immoral, but the threat itself is moral if it keeps the peace. So far it seems to have done so.

While it is comforting that deterrence can be seen as moral, it is most crucial that it seems to work. This apparent tendency for deter-rence to work is often obscured by many critics of nuclear weapons strategy. They argue that new and more dangerous weapons are con-stantly being developed as the superpowers engage in a destabilising arms race. While it cannot be denied that new weapons have been built, it is not true that the balance of terror has become less stable. The reasons for the procurement of new weapons and their implica-tions are far less conspiratorial or dangerous than the radicals of right and left suggest. Let us begin by first debunking the arms race theory which suggests the unending acquisition of 'overkill' will inevitably result in nuclear war.

THE ARMS RACE

What many people find most difficult to accept about nuclear weapons is that there are so many of them. The reasoning goes that if these bombs are so powerful, then why does each side need so many? Why do you need overkill – the capacity to kill many times over the total required to achieve your original purpose? The answer, as with many of the other issues already discussed, is not simple.

Yes, there are too many nuclear weapons; but no, their large numbers are not due to what the critics on the left simply call an arms race. We have already suggested some rational reasons for a wide variety of nuclear weapons, and we will discuss below some less rational reasons, but first it is necessary to sort out the misconceptions about arms races. To begin, it is often suggested that weapon build-ups necessarily lead to war. The theory goes that if a state has the weapons, it will inevitably use them. It is sad to see such fatalism from the otherwise idealistic supporters of the nuclear disarmament movement. Wars tend to be caused by political (or personal) forces. Politics makes use of weapons available, but weapons do not cause the conflict. As we have already suggested, the present nuclear weapons balance is rooted in a clash of ideological systems, and the massive build-up of nuclear weapons followed rather than preceded this conflict. Politics is at the core of conflict and to argue that technology determines the inevitability of war is to misunderstand the sources of policy.

Second, an arms race suggests that all weapons are as bad and indeed are of the same line of development. This is patently absurd. Some weapons are more accurate and destabilising, while others are slower, less accurate and can have no other purpose than retaliation and deterrence. In pre-nuclear, so-called arms races, few people would have argued that the development of anti-aircraft technology and bomber aircraft were both as dangerous.

The present Soviet claim that they need more tanks in Europe than NATO because of the west's advantage in anti-tank weapons rings so false precisely because we do make a distinction between offensive and defensive weapons while accepting that there are also some grey areas.

Third, not all weapons are developed in reaction to the development of other weapons. The simplistic proponents of arms races suggest there is a child-like acquisitiveness on the part of the powers to have the latest toy just because their opponent has it. There is no doubt an element of this human foible in the process of developing new weapons, but to make that the centrepiece of the argument is to miss the far more complex reasons for why nuclear weapons are developed. For one thing there is a long 'lead time' of up to ten years for many weapons, making it very difficult to find a simple action–reaction pattern of arms purchases.

As we have already suggested, many weapons are developed so as to make credible the threat to carry out assured destruction in the event of a first strike. This defensive rationale in the US has undergone several modifications precisely because it was felt that the cre-

dibility of the strategy had to be enhanced. Thus the strategic triad –
basing nuclear forces in bombers, on land and at sea – obviously suits,
and is encouraged by, bureaucratic and service rivalries in the US, but
it is a reasonable posture if it usefully enhances credibility. However,
obviously some weapons have more dangerous characteristics than
others.

Nuclear weapons on bombers are useful because they can achieve
deterrence by assured destruction but with less risk and miscalculation. The bombers can fly on alert so they cannot be as easily struck
first in a surprise bolt from the blue. They can also be recalled if sent
off on a false alarm. They are less offensive than other systems
because they take some time to get to their targets and thus are less
able to launch a surprise attack. These key characteristics of survivability, human control and second rather than first strike capability,
make bombers safer and less aggressive weapons. An arms race in
these weapons is less dangerous.

Nuclear weapons on land-based missiles used to be seen in a positive light because they could always get through to their target, thus
assuring destruction. Once loaded with solid rather than liquid fuel
they could always be ready to be fired and thus needed less warning
time in a sudden crisis. But land-based missiles have many dangerous
qualities that make them less defensive and more worrying. These
missiles are not as survivable as bombers. They can be hit by accurate
strikes by opposing missiles, and since they are fixed in silos they
cannot escape detection and targeting. Attempts to base these missiles on mobile systems have so far proven too costly. What is more,
once fired, these missiles cannot be recalled. Human choice is limited.
Perhaps the worst characteristic of land-based missiles is that they
embody the most accurate of all available technologies. This means
they can threaten to launch a disarming first strike on the enemy's
missiles and therefore make the adversary more nervous in times of
crisis.

The third leg of the triad, missiles on submarines, has mixed characteristics. Submarines lurk in distant waters,or even in protected
coastal areas where the enemy cannot locate and target them.Thus
they are, like bombers, a relatively invulnerable, second strike
weapon. They also patrol with men on board, so like aircraft they can
be recalled to port. But unlike aircraft they don't move to their target
and drop a bomb, they launch a missile that, once fired, cannot be
recalled. So submarines have some, but not all, of the positive aspects
of human control. Finally, until recently the sea-based nuclear mis-

siles were less accurate than their land-based counterparts, and therefore were less useful in a preemptive counterforce strike. Now that new technology makes submarine missiles more accurate, they are losing some of the relatively safe, second strike characteristics. Clearly, in limiting nuclear weapons in arms control, different elements of the triad require different treatment (see Chapter 2). To see all weapons as undifferentiated in an arms race is to misunderstand the grey areas of nuclear strategy.

Critics might respond that the nuclear arsenal has even more weapons than we have described and the overkill capacity is even more distressing., Of course there is overkill and many of the weapons should be reduced or eliminated, but as we have already suggested, not all are as dangerous. Let us look at some of the newer weapons and see how dangerous they might be.

Cruise missiles are unmanned bombers that move relatively slowly in complicated patterns to their targets with great accuracy. They can be launched from air, land or sea, and thus are mobile. Cruise missiles can be considered a second strike weapon because they are mobile and can survive a first strike. They travel so slowly that they are not useful as a counterforce weapon. Cruise missiles are also cheap and can be placed on board existing platforms like submarines or aircraft. In sum, cruise missiles help provide a defensive second strike.

What about star wars, where opponents fight for control of outer space? On the one hand this is a positive development because with space weapons the bombs destroy other bombs and not people. But apart from the vast cost of these as yet neophyte systems, the development of space technology can be destabilising. Because so much of modern communication designed to keep war controlled and assured destruction credible is dependent on satellites based in space, it is feared that if these systems can be incapacitated, then destabilisation and war are more likely to ensue. Thus the saving of lives by the first bombs falling in space rather than on earth might well be a false economy.

Similarly, there are the new technologies being developed to track and target the otherwise invulnerable nuclear armed submarines. These so-called 'hunter-killer' submarines are clearly destabilising since they seek to eliminate a relatively safe, second strike system. Deterrence of war is thereby weakened even though the hunter-killers might appear at first glance to be defensive. They also have roles in purely conventional conflict. They are not defensive if they eliminate another defensive system. This confusion (and yet another grey area) is even more evident when looking at other potentially defensive new technologies.

There has been a great deal of concern expressed that either the US or the Soviet Union has developed a particle beam or laser weapon that would shoot down incoming missiles and bombers by firing a beam of power at them. While no one has yet been able to make such systems work (clouds and atmosphere refract such beams), it is easy to see how revolutionary they might be if they did work. Assured destruction would no longer be assured, and the defence would once again predominate over the offence. Or at least the defence would predominate if both sides developed the system at the same time. But if only one side had such a defensive weapon, then it could threaten to destroy the enemy and protect itself, thereby obtaining real power. In the distant future such technology may mean the end of the nuclear danger by once again shifting the balance back to the defence and eliminating the threat posed by nuclear forces. But such a shift might also be the trigger for nuclear war as one power feels it has a reliable defence and the other does not. The problem of credibility remains crucial, especially when none of the technology or politics suggests anything clearer than grey area solutions.

As if these complexities were not enough to lay to rest the simplistic arms race argument, it is also clear that the different Soviet nuclear weapons doctrine provides different reasons for acquiring nuclear force. For example, since the US sees the need for a triad of forces while the Soviet Union does not, it is not reasonable to suggest a simplistic arms race between the two powers. Moscow is less concerned with its own sea-based force and therefore pursues different policies in this area. The limits of geography mean that Soviet submarines must pass through 'choke points' when leaving any of their home bases for the ocean. The western allies sit at these points tracking, and therefore reducing the survivability of the Soviet fleet. Once at sea the Soviet submarines are noisier and shorter range, both of which undercut the ability to survive detection. It is therefore perhaps not surprising that Moscow is more concerned with tracking US submarines by using the destabilising hunter-killers, when the US can carry out surveillance in other ways. It is also not surprising, then, that technological developments do not follow parallel paths.

In order to cope with their own weakness, as well as other deeper institutional and historical factors, the Soviet Union has emphasised its land-based forces. As we have already suggested, these ICBM forces are the most destabilising because they tend not to be as survivable or controllable and have accuracy leading some to believe they could be used in a first strike. What is more, until recently the Soviet forces used liquid as opposed to solid fuel so they rested on a more delicate hair trigger, vulnerable to preemptive strike. When the Soviet Union modernised its land-based forces it vastly increased its strength, especially by placing MIRVs on the missiles, and it did so in the most destabilising category of weapons. This was not necessarily for aggressive reasons. But because of the nature of the weapons, and the peculiar biases that favour these types of weapons in the Soviet Union, the effect was dangerous. This is not an arms race in the traditional sense, for it affects only a certain type of weapon and in an asymmetrical way. Given the different reasons for acquiring weapons, arms control needs a method that will emphasise the roles of weapons, i.e. limiting first strike forces, and not just the aggregate numbers as postulated in an arms race scenario (see Chapter 2).

Some cynics suggest that no control can overcome the pressures of an arms race because there is a so-called military-industrial complex driving the race. The term, first used by President Eisenhower (a military man) in his farewell address, has been much abused. Conspiracy theorists feel happier if they know that they are powerless because the huge hidden hand pulling strings absolves them of any necessity for action or even compromise. Rather than conspiracy theory, there is the cock-up theory of history, suggesting that actions result from myriad forces at work, few of which can be fully controlled. We lean to the latter view in arguing that the military and industry do have some things in common, but not always. For example, the rivalries between the three services in the US encouraged the development of a triad of American forces, and it certainly suggests that there is not a unified military position in nuclear strategy.

What is more, US strategy of assured destruction is essentially not a military theory, it is one devised by civilians, and to a large extent by academics. The notion that nuclear war cannot be fought, and does not serve as a useful instrument of policy, seriously undercuts the Clausewitzian notion that has inspired much earlier military thought. It is argued by some analysts of Soviet strategy that precisely because US deterrence strategy is a civilian and not military notion, MAD is opposed by the Soviet military. This may have a large grain of truth, but it is not proof of a Soviet military-industrial complex. Others say that the Soviet Union *is* a military-industrial complex rather than just *having* one, as in the US. Once again the conspiracy theorists underestimate the complexity of the political world. Leaving aside the important interservice rivalries in the Soviet military, there are also important cross-cutting cleavages that divide military industry from civilian industry or supporters of spending on steel rather than electronics.

In sum, there can be little doubt that there is 'overkill' in the amount of nuclear weapons. This is not the result of any conspiracy, but rather due to the differing reasons for acquiring weapons. Diverse doctrines, historical motivations, institutional pressures, budget restrictions or technological preferences all intertwine to produce the increasingly complicated superpower arsenals. Massive cuts can be made in the amount of forces without providing anyone with a rational first strike or creating dangerous instability.

But before these cuts can be outlined in greater detail, it is necessary to emphasise that the trends in weapons development have not upset the basic element; the balance of terror remains robust. This is true because despite a massive growth in redundant weapons, stability has not been significantly weakened and no side has been able to gain a useful unilateral advantage. If it is the critics of the left who seem most concerned with instability, it is the critics on the right who seem most concerned with gaining unilateral advantage. Let us look in greater detail at the idea of gaining superiority in nuclear weapons.

'WHAT IN THE NAME OF GOD IS SUPERIORITY?'

Proponents of the arms race theory tend to come from the radical left of the spectrum, arguing that simple solutions are available to halt war-mad conspirators before they lead us 'as lambs to the slaughter'. The other side of the spectrum, the radical right, tend to suggest there is a point to acquiring all these weapons because either the west needs to be superior, or the other side is seeking superiority. In a moment of deep and perceptive exasperation in 1974, Henry Kissinger asked, 'What in the name of God is superiority? What is the significance of it, politically, militarily, operationally, at these levels of numbers? What do you do with it?'

Superiority means having enough power to coerce and enough defence to avoid being coerced in return. But such superiority is an elusive goal. Additional bombs are not the answer because in the nuclear age of mutual vulnerability, more power only makes the rubble bounce. Because costs clearly outweight benefits in any conceivable scenario of nuclear war, any victory would be pyrrhic. So long as there is no effective defence against nuclear war, costs will always be too high. As we have already mentioned, the possible development of beam weapons might alter that equation of costs and benefits, but so far it is not near becoming reality.

Some suggest that the Soviet Union can speak of seeking superiority because it is not as concerned with the high costs of nuclear war, or that it can survive such a war in a way that the US cannot. While it is true that the Soviet Union spends far more on civil and air defence than does the west, there is little evidence that it is money well spent (see the arguments on civil defence below). More importantly, it is presumptuous to make the morally asymmetrical argument that the Soviet Union can bear more casualties in war than the west. The more than twenty million deaths in the Soviet Union during the Second World War were suffered gradually and they are not evidence that the Soviets could now bear to suffer such casualties at one shot. If anything, the fact that the Soviets have borne such a loss may now make them less willing to do so again than the Americans who do not appreciate what such a scale of destruction really means. Thus the suggestion that superiority has any real military meaning seems far from the truth.

There is a related argument that superiority might have political if not military meaning. Radicals of the right suggest that there is a growing window of opportunity (for the USSR) or of vulnerability (for the US) that results from the Soviet Union having the potential to launch a preemptive strike using most of its land-based missiles to wipe out the US land-based missiles. The result would be the elimination of all the accurate US forces. Thus Washington would have no weapons left that could strike limited Soviet targets and the US could only retaliate against Soviet cities. Since a counter-city strike would be an escalation, the US would refrain from responding and therefore bow to Soviet pressure. If the onus is upon the US to strike an escalatory blow, the US is said to have suffered 'escalation dominance' and is weaker politically.

This conspiracy theory of the right is deeply flawed and as such gives strategic studies a bad name. The idea that the Soviet Union could obtain such accuracy and total success flies in the face of anything that is known about the technological performance of nuclear missiles. What is more, it assumes that the US will not respond to an attack that although aimed at missiles, kills tens of millions of people in (optimistic?) collateral damage. The US, even under this nightmare of the right, still maintains two legs of its triad, with the accuracy to destroy smaller Soviet cities or larger bases. The only useful point that the argument about a window of vulnerability has to make is that some sort of invulnerable second strike accuracy is required in order to help credibly to deter such a scenario, as absurd as it may sound. In the end, credibility needs to be secured, although for all intents and purposes it probably continues to exist.

This supposed political utility of nuclear superiority is also said to be linked to non-nuclear crises. The rightwingers argue that the 1962 Cuban missile crisis was 'won' by the west because it had nuclear superiority and could force Moscow to back down. What now seems far more likely was that US conventional superiority in the Caribbean placed the onus on the Soviet Union to raise the conflict to a nuclear level – escalation dominance counts far more on the point separating conventional and nuclear war. The various Berlin crises where the Soviet Union did have conventional superiority and still did not initiate war makes an even more pacific point that the risk of any translation of military power into political power is severely circumscribed. Because there is general recognition that war between nuclear powers is so lethal it can hardly serve as a useful instrument of policy. Since nuclear superiority has no military meaning, neither can it have a political meaning.

Henry Kissinger noted in 1972 that 'we and the Soviet Union have begun to find that each increment of power does not necessarily represent an increment of usable political strength'. But if the US continuously complains about their own weakness when they are in fact strong, and denigrates their own credibility when they are in fact credible, then an increment in nuclear forces might take on political significance. Weakness could then become a self-fulfilling prophecy resulting from a self-inflicted wound. Thus the sooner that nuclear superiority is recognised as a myth and emphasis is placed on ensuring a credible deterrent by assured destruction, the easier it will be to make real progress in arms reduction. Once again it is not so much rational races of arms spending that is of concern, but more the unnecessary complication caused by spending on redundant systems and the salving of rampant conspiracy nightmares of right and left. Significant cuts can be made without damaging stability or encouraging a first strike.

Once again it is crucial to reiterate that the essentials of deterrence have not been upset by all these new weapons. It is easy to lose sight of the two bedrock elements of contemporary deterrence. First, the maintenance of sufficient forces to inflict assured destruction has not been compromised. Second, nor has the ability to respond at graduated levels of threat, even against some counterforce targets, been compromised. Deterrence holds, and will continue to do so as long as these two aspects are retained and no potentially destabilising threat of a first strike is posed to the enemy. All this can be done, and still severe cuts in the present number of nuclear weapons (for example the ICBM) can be made.

CIVIL DEFENCE

Optimists and pessimists, some radicals of the right (and a few on the left) have a somewhat mystical belief that the effects of nuclear war can be limited by passive defence measures such as civil defence. Some argue that with effective spending on civil defence, including shelters and crisis planning centres, the effects of nuclear war can be so minimised as to make it rational to expect to ride out a nuclear attack. Others take a somewhat more sophisticated view that errs on the side of pessimism. They seem to think that the Soviet Union, in an effort to reduce the costs of a preemptive nuclear strike, has evolved an effective system of civil defence. These radicals of the right argue that Moscow then has an advantage over the west as it can ride out an attack and therefore is striving towards superiority. They then assert that the west must also spend on shelters and passive defence so as to counter the Soviet threat. The Reagan administration has recently decided to spend over $4 billion on civil defence in the groundless belief that the United States' casualties can be halved as a result.

These extremists bear responsibility for perpetuating the cruel deception and suggesting the colossal waste of money involved in civil defence. We have already made clear that nuclear war is the most horrific kind of warfare imaginable. The ease with which the offence can strike and the sheer scale of damage inflicted makes any calculation that society can survive a nuclear war with anything like life as we know it a nasty hoax. In pre-Second World War strategic thinking it was argued that 'the bomber will always get through' and thus strategic bombing would be devastating. While it was true that the bomber always got through, it was unable to deliver devastating damage. Nuclear weapons now make it plain that the missile will always get through, and it will have an appalling impact. To think otherwise is to ignore the horror of nuclear war.

It is not ethnocentric to say that just because western powers do not have civil defence and the Soviet Union does, that we are right. The Kremlin *is* making a mistake. The argument is based on the clear evidence that even the Soviet Union is not satisfied with the usefulness of its civil defence programme. Despite the enormous sums spent on shelters, communication and emergency procedures, the Soviet Union is no closer to ensuring effectively that a significant portion of its population and industry can survive even a 'middle-sized nuclear war' (whatever that means in the light of the weapons' devastation). So far, technology and planning offers no protection from nuclear weapons. This may change in the future, but for now, money spent on civil defence is wasted, above and beyond easing some people's do-gooder instincts in the face of the horrors of nuclear war. In the Soviet case, the money is probably spent for a complex combination of reasons including ideology (socialism must triumph) and social control. In the west, it is argued that it is possible to 'protect and survive', but it is a false hope. It is certainly better to 'protest and survive', but even better to 'negotiate and survive'.

PROLIFERATION

One of the few questions of nuclear strategy that results in relative unanimity is how to view the spread or proliferation of nuclear weapons. While the left may claim this issue as their own in opposing the retention by Britain of nuclear weapons, the world of strategic studies is not as simplistic as that. Most supporters of the right also oppose proliferation, no doubt because it would complicate their game theories or it might be used by radicals whom they oppose in the Third World. In fact, other than the occasional eccentric theorist, the most vociferous proponents of proliferation are small states engaged in local conflict or pretentious dictators with delusions of grandeur. Even China, the state once feared as the most likely dangerous proliferator, has refused to assist others in 'going nuclear'.

Some might see this Chinese example as a reason why proliferation is not such a bad thing. It is said that certain states act dangerously because they are afraid of nuclear blackmail and if they can feel more confident about defending themselves, then they will be more cautious. Perhaps, but this seems to be a hair-raising way of achieving security. One need merely contemplate the continuing crises if Israel persists in taking out the Iraqi nuclear plant or if India decides that it would be a good thing to preempt the Pakistani project before it bears its rotten fruit. The vision of states with insecure and small nuclear forces of poor quality with inefficient command and control is not reassuring. Only secure second strike forces might help international security and that level of nuclear weapons development is not easy to obtain or maintain. Those proliferators who seek bombs in basements as insurance policies against threats, are buying useless policies.

Clearly there is a great deal of cant and hypocrisy in the arguments of the superpowers and their four colleagues in the nuclear club that proliferation should be ended and others prevented from obtaining what they already have. There is also a hint of racism in the western emphasis on the need to keep bombs out of the hands of Third World states. But there is good reason to be concerned with the proliferation of nuclear weapons, and especially to the Third World. Leaving aside the issue of whether the Third World has more lunatic leaders than the so-called developed world, it is indisputable that there are more conflicts in this part of the world.

In the nuclear age the superpowers and the developed world have seen less conflict than the Third World with its numerous and often just struggles to sort out colonial, imperial and national legacies. It is also reasonable to be concerned about a catalytic war; one that results from local states with nuclear weapons drawing in larger powers with bigger weapons. At its most basic level, if we all accept that nuclear weapons are so horrific and we try to control them, then why should anyone argue that it is useful to spread the problem around the world? Negotiations are complicated enough without adding extra uncertainties.

At the same time, it is necessary to keep in mind that proliferation need not be a cause for panic. It need be a cause for concern, but some problems are worse than others. A terrorist group in possession of a bomb would be dangerous, but it would not mean the end of the earth. It might be a rationale for a civil defence programme, if civil defence were not so expensive. Weapons have already proliferated to a certain extent without causing too much added uncertainty. China and then India spread the weapon to the east and China has been especially cautious in developing its forces. Arguably the Chinese are less dangerous (if they ever were) because they feel more secure.

Perhaps the only alternative other than effective international control of proliferation, or pious mutterings of disapproval as yet another state goes nuclear, is to press potentially nuclear states to adopt what seems to be the Israeli approach. In all probability Israel has a nuclear capability in order to deter 'the end of days', but it knows that to be unambiguous about this capability would spur its rivals to build their own bomb. So Israel has opted for a doctrine of ambiguity which says it will neither be the first nor the second state to introduce nuclear weapons to the area. This 'one and a half' doctrine helps to ensure not only deterrence but also non-proliferation. Obviously this is no guarantee that nuclear weapons will not spread but it is a step in the right direction.

In the final analysis, weapons proliferate because states feel insecure. Security, as we well know, is based on often subjective and therefore unquantifiable calculations of the adversary's capabilities and intentions. Therefore the problem is not subject to neat solutions, but on balance security is unikely to be enhanced by a proliferated world. Upon this point most debaters of nuclear strategy should find agreement. They proceed from the assumption that nuclear weapons are dangerous and that we must try to limit them as much as possible. After all, it would be best to see the superpowers' capability reduced, not the rest of the world's capability raised to the same lunatic level.

STRATEGY AND SURVIVAL

The many shades of opinion on nuclear strategy often combine elements of both optimism and pessimism. The left tends to argue pessimistically that war is inevitable, but optimistically that disarmament can work. The right tends to argue pessimistically that the Soviet Union is an ever-present threat and optimistically that nuclear war might not be such a terrible thing. The radical centre tends to be cautiously optimistic. By rejecting prophetic and indeed nearly biblical apocalyptic statements from left and right, it becomes possible to argue more positively that there is greater hope for living with and controlling many of the dangers of nuclear weapons.

We have argued that there are real dangers of nuclear weapons being used and have acknowledged that there is a crucial problem in preventing the horrors of nuclear war. But we have also made it clear that once having declared a moral position, the problem is not subject to simple solutions. Two unalterable aspects of the nuclear weapons issue make it necessary to explore the grey areas of debate. Not only can nuclear weapons not be uninvented, but, more crucially, the weapons themselves are not the problem. The central problem is that weapons are merely tools of the political process where conflict among states seems to be the norm. It would be nice to eliminate international conflict entirely, but utopian dreams in world politics have rarely had the slightest chance of fulfilment.

In the contemporary age, the central conflict is between east and west. Therefore it is not surprising that nuclear weapons play a major part in US – Soviet relations. It has been acknowledged that the depth of the nuclear weapons problem could be greatly reduced if there were no east–west clash. However, we have argued that in the western perspective the Soviet Union is a threat, against which, at a minimum, it would be prudent to maintain countervailing power.

The necessity to deter the Soviet Union includes nuclear weapons because the Kremlin has such force. But it has also been shown that competitive coexistence with the Soviet Union need not be an excuse for open-ended arms spending. Contrary to the criticisms of left and right, nuclear deterrence is stable. This means two things: there is no great likelihood of nuclear war, nor is there a real probability of one side gaining unilateral advantage.

Since a vast percentage of the present nuclear weapons are redundant to the basic need of credibly deterring an attack, major cuts can be made in the present nuclear arsenals. No reductions will completely eliminate the nuclear threat unless there is a fundamental breakthrough in weapons development, or until there is a radical change in international politics and conflict ceases to exist in any form. Even if there should be some peaceful resolution to east–west tension, the nuclear weapons problem will not disappear. But, to end on a more optimistic note, some real progress can be made in reducing the nuclear threat. Certain weapons can probably be unilaterally eliminated, but most need to be negotiated away. We have already suggested which type of weapons are more dangerous than others and hence should be the focus of negotiations. But for a more detailed analysis of the much needed 'art of the possible', we must turn to the next chapter on arms control.

2 Untying the Nuclear Knot

EDWINA MORETON

Concern over nuclear weapons is not the monopoly of today's anti-nuclear movement. Leaders of both superpowers have themselves long recognised the need to curb the growth of their respective nuclear arsenals and to nudge their competition and mutual suspicion into less deadly channels. So far this has been easier said than done. Detente – the relaxation of tensions between east and west in the 1970s – should have made the task easier. In some ways it probably did for a time. It is always easier to sit down and talk about difficult problems if a modicum of goodwill exists on both sides. The first strategic arms limitation agreement (SALT 1) was signed in 1972, just as detente was getting into full swing. Negotiations began almost immediately on a follow-up agreement, SALT 2. Yet looking back from a vantage point in the 1980s, the arms control record of the 1970s is disappointing, especially when measured against those aspects of the arms competition left unchecked and the tasks still ahead. Why?

The answer, in part, is that SALT was too easily snared in the political wrangling both within the United States and between the United States and the Soviet Union. SALT 2 was never ratified by the United States Senate and arms control talks were effectively suspended following the. Soviet invasion of Afghanistan in December 1979. Some of the treaty's critics at the time objected to the signing of any agreement with an Afghan-invading Soviet Union, some objected to signing any agreement with the Soviet Union at all, and some had all along objected to the provisions of SALT 2, claiming that they left the United States at a strategic disadvantage and so endangered American security and the strategic balance. Some of the more complex, technical reasons for slow progress in arms control negotiations are examined below. But first a political bone or two to pick with the critics of SALT.

SALT is not and should not be made to be synonymous with detente. Although the signing of SALT 1 coincided with a marked upswing in Soviet–American relations, it was not detente that gave arms control talks a shove in the right direction. If anything, it was the other way around. The first serious agreement on arms control with the Soviet Union was signed by President Kennedy in 1963: the partial test-ban treaty. It followed, not a period of detente, but a series of acute crises in east–west relations: the Berlin crisis, which had only really petered out in early 1962, and the Cuban missile crisis of October 1962, which brought the two superpowers closest yet to the point of direct confrontation since the end of the Second World War.

Why choose a time like this to begin direct arms control negotiations with the Russians? After all, Kennedy had won: he had stared the Russians out over Cuba and Khrushchev had blinked first. But it was precisely because Kennedy had come so close to the brink and had been sufficiently impressed with the risks of confrontation in the nuclear age that he was prepared to see the United States and the Soviet Union take a first step backwards from the abyss.

In other words, although periods of detente can help create a political climate which fosters faster progress in arms control talks, it is in times of tension that arms control is particularly needed. The first series of SALT talks opened in November 1969, after a delay caused by the Soviet invasion of Czechoslovakia in August 1968. One of the overriding American motives for beginning the talks, despite cool political relations between east and west, was the enormous and rapid expansion of the Soviet nuclear arsenal during the 1960s. 'Parity' of sorts with the United States was already in sight. More threatening, however, was the momentum which had built up behind the Soviet drive for strategic 'equality' and which was beginning to look unstoppable.

The point may have been drowned out by the row over the Soviet invasion of Afghanistan and threatening Soviet noises over Poland, but it is worth repeating: arms control is not and should never be seen as a political concession to either side. The purpose of arms control is to enhance security. To do its job, any arms control agreement has to be of positive advantage to both sides and be able to stand on its own merits. That is not to argue that arms control negotiations between the United States and the Soviet Union can be entirely isolated from the vicissitudes of political relations (if only because treaties have to be ratified by politicians). But if it is to enhance security and help reduce the risk of nuclear war, arms control does need considerable cushioning from external shocks. And similarly, any agreement concluded must be able to bear up just as well in the bad times as in the good.

Security from nuclear threat is a fundamental concern of both east and west. The mutual suspicion and hostility which gave rise to the accumulation of nuclear weapons in the first place mean that, should either side threaten to remove existing constraints on its own nuclear build-up, the effect is not to force the opponent to the negotiating table, but to ensure another spiral in the arms build-up on both sides. That goes as much for American pressure on the Soviet Union over SALT as for Soviet pressure on the west over nuclear weapons in Europe (see Chapter 3). In short, the stakes on both sides are too high to allow for anything other than mutual compromise or mutual competition.

Similarly, since it is ultimately in the interests of both superpowers to curb the growth in their respective nuclear arsenals, and since (as will be argued below) arms control negotiations are still the safest and most effective way to do the job, it makes no sense on either side to foreclose the 'option' of talks in order to pressure the other side into making concessions. There may be an argument for cutting off talks in the most extreme circumstances, but both sides must then reckon on undermining their own security as well as that of the opponent. A real arms race would be unwinnable and would exact an enormous toll on the domestic political and economic stability of either superpower and their allies. The Soviet economy is certainly weaker and less advanced than that of the United States. The burden of increased defence expenditure is therefore all the greater. Yet President Reagan has found Americans increasingly reluctant to take on the enormous burden of 'rearmament', especially nuclear rearmament, in peacetime. And even a temporary halt in arms control negotiations can be costly: arms control negotiations take so long and technology races ahead so fast that extra delays simply undermine the ultimate effectiveness of agreements signed.

Thus, by the end of the 1970s, arms control already had two albatrosses slung round its neck. The first was the assumption on the part of those who wanted to salvage the spirit of detente, that arms control could somehow carry the entire weight of maintaining good political relations with the Soviet Union. But arms control is not a political panacea. Those too eager to defend the virtues of arms control contributed to a misunderstanding of what it cannot do and became correspondingly disillusioned with the process. After the Soviet invasion of Afghanistan many were disappointed that talks about arms control had been unable to stop the invasion. They then lost all further interest in the talks.

The second obstacle in the way of progress in SALT 2 was the assumption that arms control talks could be made to stop and start with the ups and downs of political relations. On the very extreme of this group of SALT's critics in the United States (but also very probably in the Soviet Union too) were those whose black thoughts about the Soviet Union led them to the belief that no arms control agreement to which the Soviet Union was prepared to append its name could possibly do anything but undermine the security of the United States. To paraphrase Groucho Marx: they did not want to become members of an arms control club that would admit both superpowers as members. This unease with the whole process of negotiation with the Soviet Union deepened as the United States was forced to contemplate an end to almost three decades of measurable strategic superiority.

Yet arms control is neither a reward for favourable conduct nor an expression of moral 'trust'. Nor does it stem from common goals, save that of avoiding mutual annihilation. Negotiation over nuclear weapons does not assume that the Soviet Union has western interests at heart – or vice versa. Nor does it amount to moral disarmament. As argued above, interest in arms control has to be mutual if the result is to enhance strategic stability. And it is too important to leave to the good times – the times of highball-to-highball diplomacy rather than eyeball-to-eyeball confrontation. Strategic stability cannot be ensured entirely separately from some degree of political stability in superpower relations. But each must be negotiated as separately as possible if they are to feed back into each other positively.

The lesson may have sunk in. Despite the rhetoric of confrontation on both sides since the Soviet invasion of Afghanistan, and despite the fact that the SALT 2 agreement remains unratified, neither superpower has yet exceeded the bounds laid down in the SALT 2 treaty. President Reagan scarcely enjoys the reputation of a dove in the Kremlin, and his proposed increases in the American defence budget have made him a target of considerable Soviet abuse. Yet it has not escaped the notice of the Soviet leadership, although it has gone apparently undetected by Western Europe's 'peace' movement, that none of the provisions and ceilings in SALT 2 has been breached by the new programmes proposed to Congress so far. The Soviet Union, likewise, has pledged to observe the limits of SALT 2 provided the Americans continue to do so. Both sides have an interest in not breaking the agreement, however hostile their mutual political relations have become.

But SALT could not be put on hold forever. The longer the delay in restarting arms control talks at the strategic level, the greater the pressure on one side or the other to breach the SALT ceilings or else to go for new weapons programmes which, while they do not strictly contravene SALT 2 or whatever proposals succeed it, simply channel the arms competition into different but equally if not more deadly technologies. On 9 May 1982, President Reagan proposed that talks begin in June 1982 on strategic arms reduction (START) in place of the moribund SALT 2 treaty (see below).

WHY 'BANNING THE BOMB' WON'T HELP

Some have criticised SALT for moving too fast, some for moving too slowly. Others prefer to ignore arms control altogether in favour of what they see as being more radical solutions to the problem of nuclear weapons. After all, if the obstacles to restarting arms control negotiations are so great, and their achievements thus far so meagre, why not go for wholesale disarmament instead?

Contrary to popular belief, disarmament – as the term is used by today's 'peace' movement – is not just a more radical version of arms control. And vice versa, arms control, as understood in these pages, is not just a less ambitious version of disarmament. Nor is it being advocated here as a means of shoring up the status quo. The thinking behind arms control and disarmament does stem from a single moral root: an abhorrence of the threat of nuclear war and the use of nuclear weapons, and a desire, if humanly possible, to avoid both. But despite their common moral origins, in practice they offer radically different approaches to the problem.

Disarmament promises security through the banning of weapons. One variant suggests that by unilaterally renouncing weapons – in this case nuclear weapons – individual states can remove the threat of conflict. Arms control, on the other hand, seeks to reduce the chances of war and to reduce its ferocity, should war ever break out, not only by reducing gradually the numbers of nuclear weapons but also by controlling the development, deployment and use of different kinds of weapons along lines mutually acceptable to the protagonists. It assumes that conflict cannot be eliminated, only controlled – and that nuclear weapons cannot simply be cursed out of existence.

In a perfect world successive arms control agreements could conceivably end by reducing the numbers of nuclear weapons on either side to zero. But that assumes a change in political relations between the two superpowers that goes well beyond a desire to avoid mutual annihilation. In a less-than-perfect world, advocates of arms control accept that the complete elimination of nuclear weapons, if it can ever be achieved, will not be the first step towards peace, but the last. Strategic stability (as argued in Chapter 1) rests on deterrence – the knowledge that the use of nuclear weapons by one side will provoke a devastating retaliatory strike by the other side. Unilateral disarmament, as advocated by some groups in today's anti-nuclear movement, would seriously destabilise that nuclear balance. Far from enhancing international security it could seriously endanger peace.

Why arms control? Why not disarmament? The first argument is political. Neither the Soviet Union nor the United States has the other's political interests at heart. If they did, there would be little need for stockpiles of nuclear weapons at all. And just as obviously, there would be no need to worry about controlling them. Just as the 'hawks' on the right of the spectrum of opinion in the west, who have argued against arms control negotiations with the Soviet Union on the grounds of irreconcilable political differences between the two superpowers, are wrong, so at the other end of the spectrum the argument that nuclear weapons are the root of all conflict – and that if open to rational argument the two superpowers would simply lay them aside – is equally vacuous. The stockpiles of weapons exist because of the underlying conflict between the two sides, not vice versa.

As pointed out in the previous chapter, all methods of arms control are risky, including deterrence. Devising strategies for a set of weapons whose aim is never to be used strikes many as irrational and Kafkaesque, particularly in view of the horrific consequences if deterrence fails. That point is not in dispute. The question is: what to do about it? The philosophy of arms control is based on two premises. (1) The attempt to 'ban' nuclear weapons under present circumstances is dangerous, especially if the ban is self-imposed and unilateral. Because of the closed nature of the Soviet political system, western movements protesting at nuclear weapons can only have a one-sided impact. Technology cannot simply be unlearned. What is urgently needed are effective negotiated controls to render that technology as harmless to human civilisation as possible. The nuclear secret is out, and knowledge cannot be unlearned. Nor is it enough to ignore it. (2) Since the enormous destructive power of nuclear weapons is predominantly in the hands of two superpowers whose political, economic and social systems grate on each other, any controls have to inspire confidence on both sides. The unilateral renunciation of nuclear weapons would remove neither the threat of their use nor the underlying conflicts which cause states to threaten each other's security. Given the existence of those underlying conflicts, the most secure path to continued peace is to dismantle military insecurities step by step and create a more robust, less fragile nuclear balance at the lowest possible level of arms on both sides.

ARMS CONTROL SO FAR: THE POTHOLES

Defending arms control as a philosophy for curbing the danger of nuclear war is not the same as defending the status quo – that is a mistake common to critics of the arms control process on both the left and the right of the political spectrum. Indeed, to say that arms control as practised so far leaves much to be desired is perhaps the only point on which those engaged in the current nuclear debate – left, right and centre – agree. But having argued the case for arms control against those who see it as a concession to the Soviet Union and those who think wholesale disarmament the only alternative, the time has come to poke hard at the arms control record so far.

In light of the acrimony that has characterised much of Soviet–American relations since the Second World War, the list of arms control agreements signed by the two superpowers (in some cases along with other signatories) over the past two decades is quite impressive:

the Antarctic treaty, 1959
the Limited Test-ban treaty, 1963 (banning nuclear tests in the atmosphere, in space and under water)
the Outer Space treaty, 1967 (banning weapons of mass destruction in outer space)
the treaty of Tlatelolco, 1967 (establishing a nuclear-weapon-free zone in Latin America)
the Non-proliferation treaty, 1968
the Sea Bed treaty, 1971 (prohibiting emplacement of nuclear weapons on the sea bed)
the Biological Weapons Convention, 1972
the SALT 1 Interim Agreement, 1972

the ABM treaty, 1972
the Weaponry Convention, 1981 (restricting the use of particularly
    inhumane conventional weapons, such as napalm, etc.)

These are the agreements negotiated and ratified. Negotiation has
also produced the following three agreements which still await ratification:

the Threshold Test-ban treaty, 1974 (limiting underground mili-
    tary tests to yields of less than 150 kilotons)
the Peaceful Nuclear Explosions treaty, 1976 (setting the same
    threshold for all underground tests, including those for peaceful
    purposes)
SALT 2, 1979

But in the case of arms control agreements, as in the case of nuclear
weapons themselves, quantity is not necessarily a reliable guide to the
quality of the arms control output.

The purpose of arms control is to enhance security by alternative
means. And since all parties to any agreement are looking to enhance
their own security, arms control is exceedingly difficult to negotiate.
Any arms control agreement if it is to contribute to strategic stability
must meet three basic conditions: it must limit arms in a mutually
acceptable way taking account of both sides' neuroses, and therefore
contributing to equal security; it must be balanced, so that neither
side gains additional advantage by renouncing it and both sides have
an interest in not breaking it, whether they trust each other or not;
and it must be verifiable. Unless both sides have sufficient confidence
that the other is not able to cheat, and gain undue advantage by doing
so, an arms control agreement will increase uncertainty, rather than
diminish it. The experience of a decade of SALT talks has added a
fourth consideration: to be really effective in putting a break on arms
competition, future arms control agreements need to limit not just
numbers of weapons and warheads (although stricter limits on both
would help), but also those weapons technologies which threaten to
upset the strategic balance. By these measures the arms control
record so far looks far less impressive.

THE PARTIAL TEST-BAN TREATY, 1963

This treaty represented the first major step taken by the two superpowers to limit the effects of their competition in nuclear weapons.

There had been discussion of the idea of a comprehensive test ban at the United Nations for some time. During the 1950s there had been mounting public concern at the effects of radioactive fall-out from the testing of nuclear weapons in the atmosphere. The three nuclear weapons powers – the United States, the Soviet Union and Britain – began to investigate the possibilities of a ban on the testing of nuclear weapons and in the meantime declared a voluntary moratorium on further testing, which lasted from 1958 to 1961. The moratorium was broken first by the Soviet Union. The Soviet action was quickly followed by a resumption of testing by the United States.

In 1962 and 1963 the United Nations revived the idea of a comprehensive test ban. However, such a ban would have been impossible to enforce reliably without far more detailed monitoring, including on-site inspection, than the Soviet Union in particular was prepared to tolerate. The superpowers broke away from the multilateral discussion of comprehensive test-ban proposals at the UN and signed their own limited bilateral agreement, which prohibited the testing of nuclear weapons devices in the atmosphere, in outer space and under water. However, the agreement placed no restrictions at all on tests carried out underground.

As the treaty's critics have been quick to point out, it hardly represented a great sacrifice on either the Soviet or the American part. Both countries had probably learned as much as they could from weapons testing in the atmosphere (although the ability to test systems designed for defence against incoming missiles was hampered as a result of the treaty). Both agreed to stop doing something that neither had much interest in continuing to do anyway. Seen in purely cynical terms, the 1963 test-ban treaty was more of an environmental treaty than an arms control treaty. Limiting radioactive fall-out is no bad thing. On the other hand, by taking note of public concern over 'dirty' atmospheric tests, the treaty helped focus public attention away from the most observable sign of the continuing nuclear competition between the superpowers. The testing of nuclear devices was forced underground. So the partial test ban did less than it might have to curb nuclear weapons development and did not affect the massive build-up of nuclear weapons on both sides during the 1960s and 1970s.

Although it was a step sideways rather than a step forward for arms control, the partial test-ban treaty was a signal of progress in other ways. It was the only kind of agreement possible at the time, since the Soviet Union refused categorically to allow the kind of detailed inspection that would have enabled observers to monitor compliance with a more comprehensive test ban. And it had immense psychological importance: it demonstrated, just a few months after the Cuban missile crisis, that despite their mutual hostility the two superpowers could sit down and negotiate some limits on their competition in nuclear arms. More important, it put the issue of arms control firmly on the agenda for future talks.

STRATEGIC ARMS LIMITATION TALKS: SALT 1

The next major step forward was the opening, in 1969, of the first strategic arms limitation talks. The SALT talks were a belated attempt to cope with some of the consequences of the earlier failure to halt underground testing: the development and deployment of increasing numbers of intercontinental ballistic missiles, or ICBMs. Both superpowers had been developing missiles of this type since the 1950s; both had considerably improved their quality and increased the quantity of them since.

SALT 1 comprised two arms limitation agreements, both signed in Moscow in May 1972; the 'Interim Agreement on Certain Measures with Respect to the Limitation of Strategic Offensive Arms' and the Treaty on the Limitation of Anti-Ballistic Missiles (the ABM treaty). SALT's beginnings were modest, however the significance of SALT 1 was that it dealt with both offensive and defensive weapons and their impact on the strategic balance.

The interim agreement dealt specifically with control of offensive weapons (ICBMs) and its achievements were in many ways as modest and hesitant as its rambling title suggests. It did not so much 'limit' (by reducing their number) existing ICBM arsenals as introduce a temporary freeze, covering the period from 1972 to 1977, on the numbers of strategic ballistic missile launchers deployed or under construction on both sides (including land-based and submarine-based launchers). Nor did the agreement itself establish the exact size of the respective arsenals: instead the two sides exchanged a memorandum of understanding on the subject.

Even before the ink was dry, the agreement was under attack in the United States for having codified Soviet 'superiority', instead of strategic parity in nuclear weapons. Superficially the criticism was correct: the Soviet Union already had more ICBM launchers than the United States and so would preserve that lead under the terms of the agreement. On the other hand, since the United States was not obliged to cancel any planned weapons programmes as a result of SALT 1, and since the momentum in weapons deployment had earlier been with the Soviet Union, the agreement could fairly be called an arms control agreement. SALT 1 could be more fairly criticised for limiting only launchers and not warheads too. At the time, the United States was far ahead of the Soviet Union in equipping its missiles with the ability to deliver several warheads at a time – MIRVs were first introduced into the American strategic arsenal in 1964. This lead more than counterbalanced the Soviet lead in numbers of launchers. It has since been claimed by some of SALT's critics on the liberal end of the spectrum in the United States that the SALT 1 negotiators, being fainthearted, missed a golden opportunity to nip the development of MIRV technology in the bud by restricting it while the United States had the technological lead. However it is unlikely the Soviet Union would have negotiated such a deal. The Soviet Union did not deploy its first MIRVed launchers until 1973.

A more trenchant criticism is that the interim agreement did little for arms control, precisely because it allowed both the Soviet Union and the United States to continue their competition unchecked in improving the accuracy and fire-power of the missiles they had. However, it was an 'interim' agreement and negotiations were soon underway on a follow-up treaty, SALT 2.

THE ABM TREATY

In the meantime, although the competition in offensive weapons raced ahead, defensive weapons came in for more direct scrutiny. If either side were able to devise a system which could reliably protect its own weapons and population from retaliatory attack, the incentive to launch or threaten a first strike against the opponent's weapons or population would be greatly increased. Thus, purely defensive weapons could destabilise the strategic balance by significantly altering the calculation of risk and therefore of deterrence. By prohibiting the development of such a comprehensive anti-ballistic missile defence, the ABM treaty was a first real shot in the arm for the cause of intelligent arms control. As amended at a summit meeting between Presidents Nixon and Brezhnev in 1974, the treaty limits both sides to ABM defence of one site only: the Soviet Union has an ABM network protecting Moscow; the United States earmarked its ABM network for protection of one of its ICBM sites (although the work on the system was discontinued).

As usual, the superpowers had several quite mercenary reasons for signing such a treaty. At the time it had proved technically impossible anyway to construct a fully effective ABM defence (although the United States was ahead of the Soviet Union in this particular branch of technology). And even if hypothetically feasible, the economic cost would have been prohibitive. But even recognising these baser motives, the ABM treaty showed that the two sides had learned an important lesson. Technology does not stand still. By agreeing not to exploit a technological development that could undermine the concept of deterrence, the two sides had acted early to head off a potentially destabilising development before either side was in a position to exploit a potential lead. Unlike the interim agreement on offensive missiles, the ABM treaty has no time limit. New technologies now threaten the treaty (see below), but it would be a major setback to arms control if it were lost.

THE SECOND STRATEGIC ARMS LIMITATION TREATY, SALT 2

Thus far attempts to control defensive systems had worked better than attempts to control offensive weapons. However, there were encouraging signs that both sides felt they had a mutual interest in not breaking existing agreements and in continuing the process of arms control. The second strategic arms limitation agreement, SALT 2, was a not altogether successful attempt to come to grips with some of the issues left open in SALT 1. When the SALT 1 interim agreement expired in October 1977, negotiations were already well underway on a new agreement to replace it. Until the new agreement was ready to be signed both the United States and the Soviet Union agreed not to breach the – admittedly scarcely onerous – provisions of SALT 1. Some of the basic principles to govern SALT 2, such as the principle this time of equal ceilings on strategic launchers in the different categories, had already been laid down at a meeting between President Ford and President Brezhnev in Vladivostock in 1974. SALT 2 was eventually signed in the presence of Presidents Carter and Brezhnev in Vienna on 18 June 1979. It had several components: a treaty lasting until 1985; a protocol due to expire at the end of 1981, governing key problems not resolved in the main treaty; and a joint statement of principles to govern talks leading to SALT 3.

The SALT 2 treaty was not perfect. Again sharply attacked by critics in the United States (and, it seems, in the Soviet Union too), the new treaty stood at least a sporting chance of ratification by the

United States Senate until the Soviet invasion of Afghanistan in December 1979, when further consideration of the treaty was suspended by President Carter.

Was it worth passing anyway? Under the provisions of SALT 2 each side would be limited to an overall ceiling of 2400 strategic launchers (delivery vehicles) until the end of 1980, and thereafter to 2250. Launchers exceeding this total were to be dismantled by the end of 1981. According to figures appended to the treaty – a snapshot of the strategic balance as of 1 November 1978 – the United States would be required to dismantle 34 launchers and the Soviet Union 254 in order to comply with the final overall ceiling (although in individual categories of weapons, both sides still had some considerable room for expansion).

Other important sub-ceilings below this overall ceiling of 2250 were applied. In a first attempt to come to grips with the proliferation of MIRVed (multi-warhead) missiles, both sides were limited to a maximum of 1320 MIRVed ballistic missile launchers (land-based ICBMs, submarine-based SLBMs and air-launched ASBMs) and heavy bombers equipped with long-range air-launched cruise missiles (ALCMs). Of this subtotal, a maximum of 1200 could be MIRVed ballistic missile launchers (either ICBMs, SLBMs or ASBMs). And of this subtotal, a maximum of 820 could be land-based ICBMs. Under the successive sub-ceilings of SALT 2 both sides were additionally to be limited to the deployment of one new ICBM each; there could be no increase in silo size and no conversion of light ICBMs to heavy ICBMs.

Rather like the Russian matroshka dolls, which fit nearly inside one another, there was a certain logic behind the progressive limits set by SALT 2. Just as the Russian dolls get smaller and smaller as each one is opened to find another doll inside, these subtotals were designed to set strict limits on the number of powerful and highly accurate land-based ICBMs in each side's strategic forces. But also like the matroshka dolls, at the end there is always one left which cannot be cracked open, no matter how small: the ICBM problem was to plague the SALT process none the less.

Neither the sceptics of the right, nor those of the left, were impressed with SALT 2. The criticisms of the agreements were both technical and general. By far the most damning was that SALT 2 did nothing to control the growth of weapons stockpiles on either side. The charge is largely true. The overall ceiling and sub-ceilings were deliberately set high to make agreement easier. In total some 300 launchers were to be dismantled. Yet these were inevitably to be the obsolete old ones, not the shiny new ones.

More important, although the treaty limited the number of MIRVed missiles to equal numbers on both sides, MIRV technology had not yet been fully developed, especially on the Soviet side, and these sub-ceilings were deliberately set to leave considerable leeway for both superpowers to MIRV more of their existing launchers and so increase dramatically the number of warheads while still observing the restrictions of SALT 2. Under the terms of the treaty, at the point of signing in 1979, the United States would still be allowed to increase the numbers of its missiles with MIRV capability by approximately 15 per cent and the Soviet Union by approximately 60 per cent. In the deadly category of land-based ICBMs the United States could still increase the number of its MIRVed missiles by 50 per cent and the Soviet Union by 35 per cent. One new statistic sums it up: in November 1969, on the eve of SALT, the ratio of American to Soviet warheads on strategic systems was roughly 2300 to 1400: in 1981, after more than a decade of SALT, the ratio was roughly 9000 to 6000.

In the light of such statistical evidence it might seem ludicrous that SALT 2 could also be attacked for being too restrictive. But it was – attacked, that is. Limits that to some were too lax, to others appeared to place a straight-jacket on America's ability to defend itself. The most extreme opponents of SALT 2 on the right argued that SALT had done nothing to ward off the Soviet threat and had failed to prevent the Soviet Union's spectacular missile build-up in the 1970s. In fact, since the SALT 2 treaty this time bound the two sides to common ceilings, it codified a shift from an earlier position of American superiority in the 1960s to a position of rough strategic parity. (Although the Soviet strategic arsenal combined greater crude explosive power, the United States held the lead in missile accuracy.)

But the issue that might have killed SALT 2 even if the Soviet invasion of Afghanistan had not happened was that of 'ICBM vulnerability' and the 'window of opportunity' that SALT 2's critics claimed the treaty would afford the Soviet Union to wipe out America's land-based ICBMs in a disarming first strike. But if the maximum number of strategic launchers, and, within that figure, the maximum number of the most accurate and lethal category, land-based ICBMs, allowed to each side under the treaty are equal, why all the fuss?

Part of the reason for concern lies in the nature of the weapons themselves. Land-based ICBMs are highly accurate: with improvements in yield and accuracy over the years, their most modern versions can strike accurately at the missiles of the other side. The 308 heavy land-based ICBMs in the Soviet armoury are already reputed to be able to destroy the smaller American land-based ICBMs in their silos. Land-based ICBMs are not only the most accurate, they are also the most vulnerable weapons in the strategic armoury, and therefore the most destabilising to the strategic balance. They sit in fixed silos, as immovable targets for incoming missiles. Unlike submarines and even aircraft, they are easy to find. With developments in offensive technology they have become increasingly vulnerable to attack. Because of these vulnerabilities, once warning of an enemy missile attack is received they must either be launched on warning or else run the risk of being lost in the strategic exchange. They therefore sit on a hair trigger. Unlike submarines or aircraft out on patrol, they cannot be recalled if the warning proves to be false. Not only are they potential first strike weapons which can threaten the missile force of the other side, but also their vulnerability in turn to enemy attack makes them even more destabilising to the strategic balance. Unlike submarine-launched or air-launched missiles they cannot be held in reserve as second strike weapons, available for retaliation.

But the main argument against SALT seems to have been less about the level of weaponry allowable than that which existed in practice at the time SALT 2 was signed. The Soviet Union already had more land-based ICBMs than did the United States, and would still have once the superfluous systems had been dismantled as the treaty stipulated. The reason is that close to 75 per cent of Soviet strategic forces are land based, compared with 25 per cent for the United States. The United States has relied more heavily than the Soviet Union on aircraft, and particularly submarines, which form a substantial part of the overall strategic triad of American forces (see Chapter 1). In part the triad was a rationalisation after the fact of a degree of competition among the different branches of the American armed forces. However the greater reliance on submarines and aircraft has become a deliberate element of American nuclear policy, in part also because such forces are more reliable as second strike weapons and less vulnerable to enemy attack. They therefore lend a greater degree of stability to the strategic balance.

Because of the larger number of the more accurate land-based ICBMs in the Soviet force, and in view of the silo-busting capabilities of the Soviet Union's heavy missiles, theoretically by the early 1980s the Soviet Union could have wiped out approximately 90 per cent of the American land-based missiles in a first strike. This was the 'window of opportunity' which so alarmed some of SALT's opponents (see Chapter 1).

On the surface of it, the calculus seems by any rational stretch of the imagination incredible. More worrying, though, would be the political impact on the United States government of a Soviet threat of such a strike. Would the Soviet Union be prepared to threaten and, if so, would the United States hold firm? This is the real dilemma of deterrence. No one knows if it will work.

However, other aspects of the problem can be handled with more certainty. If such a 'window of opportunity' existed in practice, not just in theory, it was neither created nor perpetuated by SALT. Even under the provisions of SALT 2, with their restrictions on numbers of launchers and numbers of MIRVed missiles in the different categories, the window, such as it was, could have been closed at any time by national decision. Lack of will for national defence is not an argument against SALT. The Soviet Union's heavy missiles were an additional threat to American silos that the United States nuclear forces could not match at least until such time as the United States deployed its own new MX missile and the MK 12A warheads on its Minutemen force (the MK 12A warhead is reported to have twice the accuracy and double the explosive power of existing Minuteman III warheads). Despite attacks on the failure to reduce their number in SALT 2, the Pentagon had never found such heavy missiles worth deploying for purposes of American security (and they were evidently left out of further consideration in SALT 2 in return for the exclusion of American forward-based aircraft in Europe). By the end of the decade, the modernisation of American land-based and sea-based ICBMs would have more than compensated for any advantage the heavy missiles had given the Soviet Union in throw-weight. The 'window of opportunity' could then swing open on the Soviet Union.

In any case ICBM vulnerability acts both ways. By basing such a large proportion of its strategic missile force in fixed silos on land, the Soviet Union has left itself vulnerable to American attack. With improvements in American missile technology, a successful disarming strike against the Soviet Union's equally vulnerable land-based missiles would leave the Soviet Union with something much closer to 75 per cent, rather than 25 per cent, of its missile force destroyed.

(Ironically, during SALT the Americans had been gently nudging their Soviet counterparts to put a greater percentage of their missiles out to sea, precisely because this would make the resulting balance less vulnerable to surprise attack and therefore more stable.)

Finally, it is worth noting that, from an American point of view, without SALT 2 the 'window of vulnerability', such as it was, could have been opened wider and held open longer. By imposing an upper limit on the number of warheads the Soviet Union would in practice eventually be able to deploy, SALT 2, like SALT 1 before it, put a check on the momentum of Soviet weapons production. The MX missile – the potentially mobile new missile system under development in the United States at the time and billed as capable of closing the 'window of opportunity' – would have been rendered far more vulnerable without such limits on Soviet warheads. (Although mobile missiles were limited by the protocol to SALT 2, this was due to expire in 1981, well before MX was due to be deployed. And in the end SALT proved to be the last obstacle to the deployment of a mobile ICBM system.) In sum, SALT imposed limits where none would have existed; it capped Soviet arms production momentum. It did not cap the technology race, but the United States was far better placed than the Soviet Union to take advantage of SALT's biggest loophole.

Although SALT 2 can be attacked for not having done enough to restrict the technology competition between the two superpowers at the strategic level, it caused more than a hiccough in relations between the United States and its allies in Europe, because of some very limited restrictions on the deployment of cruise missiles and on the transfer of cruise missile technology to other states. Cruise missiles (pilotless jet aircraft capable of flying at very low altitudes and closely following the terrain to avoid detection) presented too thorny a problem to be dealt with in detail under SALT 2. However, cruise missile technology was of direct interest to the West Europeans, contemplating the growing threat from the deployment of new Soviet intermediate-range missiles (SS-20s) targeted on Western Europe. Although the protocol was of relatively short duration, the row and its repercussions live on (see Chapter 3).

Reinforcing fears at the loss of a clear American edge in nuclear weapons was the fear that the Russians could not be trusted even to observe the limits the treaty did impose. One criticism of SALT 2 with potentially far-reaching consequences was that the agreement was unverifiable and therefore undermined strategic stability. Is the charge true? The Soviet Union had continued to resist detailed on-site monitoring of weapons installations, so that verification of the SALT accords has been by what is known in arms control jargon as 'national technical means', i.e. satellite reconnaisance and other forms of intelligence-gathering. Such intelligence-gathering techniques can be astonishingly accurate. However, because of possible ambiguities which can result from such forms of verification, it was decided early on in the SALT process to establish a Standing Consultative Commission (SCC) to discuss any charges by either side of violations of the SALT accords. Since the SCC was set up, in December 1972, it has met twice annually, although its proceedings are normally kept secret.

It is a reflection of the importance now attached to the SCC that, despite the suspension of arms control talks in December 1979, both President Carter and, with some hesitation, President Reagan have continued to send teams. In its short history it has defused a number of accusations of cheating on both sides and is considered by those who took part under the Nixon, Ford and Carter administrations to be an important channel for building confidence in the arms control process. Ambiguities raised had all been satisfactorily resolved There was a brief flurry of concern during the Reagan transition when it was announced that some 25–30 new Soviet violations of SALT were to be raised at the SCC. These turned out to be questions already thoroughly aired by the SCC. Press reports in April 1982, that the Soviet Union had violated SALT 2 by deploying 200 mobile ICBMs, have also been denied as false.

But the SCC's job is to monitor compliance with the treaties as concluded. Are the agreements themselves sound? Under the provisions of SALT 2, telemetry encryption – i.e. the coded transmissions of information from missile tests – is allowed except when it 'impedes verification of compliance' with the provisions of the treaty. Coding of missile test information breeds mistrust and since the information is encoded and by definition unreadable by the other side, it is impossible to be 100 per cent certain that the coding is not in violation of the treaty. Ironically, although the treaty has been attacked for this rather loose provision, the loophole was apparently favoured at the time by military and intelligence experts on both sides. It is, however, potentially open to some abuse. Both sides make use of it, but the Soviet Union uses it more than the United States. To prevent false alarms there is a good case for rewording this clause in any renegotiation of SALT 2 to ban encryption of telemetric information transmitted during tests of those missiles systems limited by the treaty.

So, on balance, was SALT 2 good or bad for arms control? A case can be made that without the two SALT agreements the strategic balance would be even less stable than it is today. There is nothing in either SALT 1 or SALT 2 to prevent the United States closing any 'window of opportunity' it felt existed. ICBM vulnerability is a problem for both sides. Because of their accuracy, speed in reaching their target and inflexibility of control and launch, land-based missiles remain the most threatening, most vulnerable and least stable element of the balance. Short of removing them altogether (see below), they will continue to frustrate the best intentions of arms controllers. However the problem was not created by SALT, which at least introduced upper limits on the numbers of these weapons.

The criticism that the number of warheads increased dramatically during a decade of SALT talks is irrefutable. It points to a core problem in the two superpowers' approach to arms control so far. Since agreement has to come from two sides – each viewing the other with hostility and mistrust – arms control agreements can only venture as far as the two sides are prepared to take them. And since both sides see arms control as a way of enhancing their own security, any concession during negotiation can always be interpreted by the sceptics as having shifted the balance in the opponent's favour. That is, if agreement can be reached at all. SALT 2, with some relatively minor adjustments, probably represented the best agreement obtainable at that stage. There is evidence, given the momentum behind arms production on the Soviet side – and the likely spiralling effect that could have produced in the west – that SALT 2 has had a restraining effect. The charge that only obsolete systems are to be dismantled as a result of the treaty overlooks the fact that even these weapons are still lethal. The upper limit on MIRVed systems, although set high, arguably has brought a degree of confidence and stability to the strategic balance and, if it continues to be observed by both sides, may have prevented an even more virulent proliferation of warheads in the future.

If that argument sounds weak, it is because the two superpowers are still very much at the start of the arms control process, not the end. Until the two sides could demonstrate to each other that they were capable of implementing some limits on arms, more radical cuts in nuclear weapons would probably have required a greater degree of mutual confidence than existed at the time. The Soviet Union and the United States remain in every sense adversary powers. Since there is no reason for either one to 'trust' the other's good intentions, confidence in arms control measures has to be built up slowly and by demonstration. If a limited arms control agreement cannot be made to work, there is no hope for a more comprehensive settlement.

Confidence-building – at least between those who believe in the arms control process – has probably been the biggest contribution of SALT so far. Only the ABM treaty (along with the outer space treaty and the non-proliferation treaty), which took the opportunity to limit the application of a technology while it was still in its early stages, could be considered an intelligent piece of arms control. Psychologically, SALT reinforced for both superpowers the idea that arms control talks and arms reductions could contribute to national security.

Where SALT falls down, at least as it has been pursued so far, is because technology races ahead in leaps and bounds, whereas arms control talks have proceeded at a snail's pace. So far SALT has concentrated on a static count: limiting numbers of launchers and – much less successfully – numbers of warheads. These have the advantage of being easy to quantify. But 'bean-counting' not only encourages the two sides to equate the level of their own security with possession of the maximum number of launchers or warheads permissible in each category, thereby encouraging a process of 'levelling up'; it also focuses attention on the asymmetries between the two sides in the different categories rather than the strategic missions the weapons are there to accomplish. And it leaves entirely unchecked the qualitative improvements in weapons accuracy and yield, which can themselves upset the purely numerical calculation of the strategic balance. The limits imposed so far have simply had the effect of directing the competition into new, but just as deadly channels.

The criticism is a valid one. The problem again is: where to from here? There is a temptation among critics of SALT from both ends of the spectrum to throw up their hands in mock despair and insist there is no future for arms control. Arms control's basic problem is that the adversary posture of the two superpowers is retained throughout the negotiations – something the 'disarmament now' lobby finds it convenient to ignore. But arms control is an integral element of both Soviet and American foreign and defence policy. Arms control does have a future. But if it is ever to realise its potential for securing the nuclear peace, it needs to readjust its focus and be bolder.

ARMS CONTROL IS NOT EASY

Two serious flaws have marred the arms control effort so far: first, in numerical terms, arms control agreements have put only the loosest of limits on the nuclear arsenals of both sides, thereby in some cases leaving considerable room for further expansion. Given the underlying hostility that has projected the two superpowers into arms competition in the nuclear age, successful imposition of these loose constraints has been no mean feat. All the same, the criticism is well directed. The number of weapons on either side allowable under SALT 2 is set at an arbitrary figure, determined in relation to existing stockpiles not some independent yardstick of stability and equal security. Future arms control agreements should be able to make the constraints bite deeper.

Second, the imposition of numerical limits has simply helped to channel competition into new technologies, as yet unlimited by SALT. Improvements in accuracy, reliability and yield can themselves destabilise the strategic balance without adding a single new weapon to the existing stockpile. If the arms competition is to be effectively blunted, arms control must encompass, not just numbers of weapons, but their quality too. And where possible, new technologies must be controlled before they add a new twist to the arms spiral.

These two weaknesses in the arms control process have fed into the popular debate on nuclear weapons. To those who resolutely oppose negotiated settlements with the Soviet Union these flaws have provided an excuse for attacking SALT. To those who would prefer to curse nuclear weapons out of existence, they have reinforced the belief that it is the conspiracy of two superpowers that keeps the nuclear arms effort going. To those in the middle, who are no less concerned over the nuclear issue, they have added pressure for more radical action to halt the growth in numbers of nuclear weapons and their increasingly deadly sophistication. After all, why pour money and energy into achieving a balance at the highest level of arms; why not go for a balance at the lowest level possible instead? In recent months several quite bold initiatives have been put forward to break arms control out of its debilitating pre-cast mould. Bearing in mind the requirements of sensible arms control, some are more worthy than others of further consideration.

HOW TO BE RADICAL AND WRONG

The two most obvious radical solutions to the central dilemma posed by the SALT negotiations are either a complete freeze, numerically and technologically, on Soviet and American nuclear forces roughly at current levels or else a radical reduction in the numbers of launchers and warheads available to either side, or both.

WHY NOT JUST FREEZE?

A complete freeze on the strategic arsenals of both sides, its proponents argue, would tackle the tricky problem of how to prevent the arms competition being rechannelled into new areas and new technologies as yet unrestricted by the more conventional SALT 1 and SALT 2 agreements. It would also prevent the two sides from deliberately increasing their nuclear arsenals beyond their requirements in order that superfluous or obsolete weapons can be used as bargaining chips in future negotiations to wring new concessions at the negotiating table.

The idea seems simple and straightforward. But would such a freeze meet the conditions for sensible arms control? The first obstacle is that a freeze has to be negotiated, it cannot simply be declared. In order to be fully comprehensive and effective, and in order for both sides to feel confident that the other was not stealing a march in secret, a nuclear freeze would presumably have to include:

1. a halt to the production of nuclear weapons-grade fissile material;
2. a halt to the flight-testing of all nuclear delivery vehicles;
3. a halt to all nuclear explosions;
4. a freeze on further production of nuclear weapons.

Taken together, these elements would go a long way towards preventing the development of new weapons and the deployment of weapons now at the development stage. But could such a freeze be enforced and reliably monitored? A ban on flight-testing might be quite easy to monitor, and could in itself be a worthwhile piece of arms control since it would put a serious crimp in new weapons development programmes. But neither a comprehensive test ban, nor a halt on the production of weapons-grade fissile materials can as yet be verified with sufficient certainty to ensure that a real freeze is being observed. The stakes are too high to allow much room for ambiguity.

The 1963 partial test ban was signed in large part because the signatories had little further use for atmospheric testing, because the fall-out was causing public concern and because of the problems involved in verifying a more comprehensive test ban. Since the Soviet Union refused to allow on-site inspection, a ban on underground testing was impractical, because unverifiable. Without on-site inspection, below a certain yield a small underground nuclear explosion is almost impossible to distinguish from natural phenomena such as earthquakes. And without agreement to some form of random inspection, rather than fixed site inspection, suspicion on both sides of cheating could not be disproved.

The problem of verification still thwarts a comprehensive test ban, although very considerable progress has been made. In 1974 the United States and the Soviet Union concluded a threshold test-ban treaty, limiting all weapons tests conducted underground to a maximum yield of 150 kilotons. The agreement has yet to be ratified. In 1976 a comparable agreement was concluded limiting peaceful nuclear explosions to a maximum yield of 150 kilotons. There is a good argument for ratifying both threshold test-ban treaties, so that verification procedures can be established and data collected. During the negotiations some significant progress was registered on the vexing issue of monitoring compliance with the agreement. The Soviet Union agreed to give up its previous opposition to on-site inspection and to allow unmanned monitoring stations to be set up on its territory, with some provision for manned monitoring of pre-designated sites. It may well prove possible to refine the limits of such agreements down to a maximum 3–5 kiloton yield without seriously undermining the ability to monitor compliance with the treaty. But below that level, without agreement on random monitoring of some sort, compliance can still not be verified with sufficient confidence Even such a refined limit would fall short of a verifiable comprehensive test ban. A freeze on all nuclear testing would immediately raise the stakes for successful circumvention of agreements. Unless both sides can feel confident that the other cannot easily circumvent the agreement, the effect is to destabilise the balance, not make it more secure.

Similar problems of verification affect the ban on the production of weapons-grade fissile material. The safeguards and monitoring system developed by the International Atomic Energy Agency are supposed to prevent the spread of nuclear weapons capability to emergent nuclear powers. However, they are sufficiently unreliable already to have raised serious doubts about their effectiveness. Looking for the small amounts of weapons-grade material needed to manufacture a nuclear bomb is already like looking for a needle in a haystack. Given the much larger nuclear capability of the two superpowers, it would be impossible. Doubts about IAEA safeguards were part of the reason for Israel's raid on the Iraqi nuclear reactor in 1981. The consequences of similar doubts at superpower level would be catastrophic, especially since the advantage to be gained from cheating and therefore the uncertainties would be enormous.

Difficulties in verifying a ban on further weapons development are matched by inherent difficulties in freezing numbers on each side. Because the arms competition takes the form of a set of spirals, rather than a race, the two sides are seldom at the same place at the same time. A freeze would sanctify such imbalances, especially in the European theatre (see Chapter 3). It would both fail to reduce the numbers of weapons and at the same time draw upon itself the fire of those who have already rejected SALT as having handed over strategic superiority to the Soviet Union. Finally, it is worth repeating the obvious: a nuclear freeze has to be negotiated if it is to contribute to stability; it cannot simply be declared without complex rules for verification.

In short, a nuclear freeze is unworkable at the present time because it is unverifiable. However it does throw up useful ideas which could and should be followed up – such as limits on flight-testing and greater restrictions on nuclear testing underground. A freeze is not itself a solution to the arms limitation dilemma and the search for strategic stability. Advocates of a freeze argue persuasively that unless radical steps are taken soon, technological developments will render verification even less secure in the future. There is logic to the argument but the answer to the problem may have to be less complex than the attempt to negotiate and verify a complete freeze.

THE WRONG CUTS CAN HURT

Noticeable cuts in the numbers of weapons on both sides would help to win some support for the cause of arms control. Combined with some means of limiting the development of new technologies and more sophisticated warheads, such as limits on flight-testing and underground nuclear explosions, cuts could make some headway in slowing down the nuclear arms competition. The stabilisation of the nuclear balance at a lower level would be a very welcome achievement. But cuts also have to be handled carefully if they are not to upset the strategic balance.

How can a reduction in the number of nuclear weapons make the nuclear balance less stable? One extreme example might be the proposal by George Kennan for an immediate, across-the-board reduction by 50 per cent in the nuclear arsenals of both superpowers. The proposed cuts would apply to all categories of weapons from long-range strategic systems, to intermediate-range weapons and tactical weapons for use in limited battlefield zones. The precise numerical calculation of what the Kennan cuts would mean has been done elsewhere. The purpose here is simply to explore some of the principles involved. Stated that baldly, at the strategic level a 50 per cent cut across the board means a reduction in the number of military targets incoming enemy warheads need to hit for an effective first strike attack. Depending how the cuts are apportioned on either side a first strike may even become a more feasible proposition, especially if the present proportions of vulnerable, land-based ICBMs are preserved on either side and the numbers of warheads available to each side are not strictly limited.

Such a radical cut also emphasises the complication to the strategic balance of the independent deterrents of Britain, France and China. The importance of these small but lethal forces grows as significant reductions are contemplated in the strategic balance at superpower level. Any Soviet pressure in negotiations of this kind for the United States to make compensation for the Soviet need to face an additional nuclear threat from a hostile China could succeed at Europe's expense, where the Soviet Union already has considerably superior forces in the shape of its SS-20 missiles already in place (see Chapter 3). And above a certain level, radical cuts in strategic forces put considerable responsibility for the maintenance of security on the conventional balance. Yet NATO in Europe has in the past consciously constructed its conventional forces to slot into an overall nuclear framework. The result would be to reveal some important deficiencies in conventional capabilities in Europe. That is not an attempt to make a case against reductions per se. The long-term aim, after all, is stable deterrence based on the minimum force necessary on each side. But across-the-board cuts create their own anomalies and instabilities. Some of these may matter more than others but enough will matter to impede a negotiated agreement.

Beyond a certain point, without a more complex agreement making major alterations to the composition of forces on both sides, and without greater control over weapons technology, massive cuts in strategic arsenals would exaggerate still further existing ambiguities and instabilities in the present balance. And unless such major altera- tions in force structures could be seen as a likely outcome of any negotiations, even the proposal of massive cuts, however sincerely meant, is likely to be seen by the other side as at best a self-serving propaganda ploy and at worst as an effort to undermine strategic stability.

This appears to have been the Soviet response to President Carter's proposals for substantial cuts in strategic forces in March 1977. The Carter proposals were admittedly badly prepared and were presented to the Soviet Union with little or no groundwork in the middle of a negotiation process whose basic principles had been agreed upon much earlier. Unlike Kennan's 50 per cent cuts, all Carter was pro- posing was a reduction in the number of delivery vehicles previously agreed at Vladivostock from 2400 to between 1800 and 2000; MIRVed launchers would be reduced from 1320 to between 1100 and 1200. The Carter figures meant a maximum of 550 MIRVed ICBMs on either side and a reduction in the number of Soviet heavy missiles from around 300 to 150. The agreement would also have permitted cruise missiles with a range of less than 2500 km in return for a ban on testing and deployment of any new ICBMs, including the United States MX missile.

The proposal was not only sprung on the Russians without prepara- tion, it threatened an unbalanced (from a Soviet point of view) reduc- tion in the Soviet Union's strong suit – heavy missiles. It was rejected out of hand as a one-sided propaganda ploy and in the end served only to slow down the eventual conclusion of SALT 2. On second glance, and particularly in view of the uncertainties created by the failure of SALT 2 to achieve ratification, the Soviet Union may have regretted dismissing the Carter proposals out of hand. The proposals were immediately withdrawn and ironically became ammunition for SALT's more hawkish critics in the United States, by providing a numerical yardstick of SALT 2's failure to cut into the Soviet heavy missile arsenal.

STRATEGIC ARMS REDUCTION TALKS (START)

President Reagan has since revived the principle of deep cuts, in part to spike growing opposition from the 'freeze' movement in the United States to his handling of arms control. The high ceilings set by

SALT 2 had been the basis of much of the criticism of the treaty anyway. In a speech in Eureka, Illinois, on 9 May 1982, President Reagan outlined a proposal to begin strategic arms reduction talks (START) with the Soviet Union in place of the unratified SALT 2 treaty. The decision to reopen arms control talks with the Soviet Union was immediately welcomed by America's European allies and, encouragingly, by the Soviet Union. The talks began in Geneva on 29 June 1982. However the START proposals have run into snags too.

The START proposal envisaged in a first phase a common ceiling of 850 long-range missiles, down according to American estimates from current levels of roughly 2350 missiles for the Soviet Union and 1700 for the United States. These 850 missiles on each side would be allowed to carry a total of no more than 5000 nuclear warheads – a reduction, according to American estimates, of roughly one-third on current totals of approximately 7500 on each side. Of those 5000 warheads no more than 2500 could be carried by land-based missiles. The reduction in land-based forces would affect the Soviet Union more than the United States; the limit on warheads would put greater restrictions on the American side. The proposal to cut missile and warhead numbers is matched in a second phase by a proposal to achieve equal throw-weight, which again would place greater restrictions on the Soviet missile force as presently deployed.

The proposal has some merit. And at least this time the proposals were not rejected out of hand by the Russians. But do they plug those loopholes left open by SALT 2? For the first time the proposals contain strict limits on total numbers of warheads, not just launchers. And they aim to restrict the most destabilising category of weapons, land-based ICBMs. In the long run they are designed to encourage the Soviet Union to put a greater proportion of its missiles out to sea, thereby emphasising their second strike, rather than their first strike qualities (although increasingly second strike submarine-launched missiles are no less lethal than their land-based counterparts). The combined throw-weight and warhead restrictions are designed, too, to encourage the Soviet Union to dispense with its destabilising multi-warhead 'heavy' missiles. A small missile force equipped with large numbers of warheads per missile is always more easily damageable than a force whose warheads are more widely dispersed among larger numbers of smaller missiles.

However, measured against the criteria for sensible arms control, START, as outlined so far, has loopholes. It fails to deal specifically with other weapons, such as submarine- and air-launched missiles. Nor does it address the complex problem of cruise missiles. However, since President Reagan has insisted that nothing is to be excluded from consideration in START, ways may yet be found to cover these important gaps in the original proposal.

Nor does START address the question of the technology race. If START takes as long to negotiate as SALT did before it – a prospect which unfortunately cannot be ruled out – both sides run the risk that the weapons they are seeking to limit, the balance they are trying to secure and the means for verifying those limits will have been outstripped by a surge of new technologies (see below).

More disturbing still, at first glance the START proposals fail to close the 'window of vulnerability' which was the centrepiece of the Reagan criticisms of SALT 2. Although the START proposals would reduce the numbers of highly accurate Soviet missiles aimed at American land-based missiles, the number of targets they have to take out on the American side would also be reduced. Thus the total effect of START as proposed so far would be to leave the disproportion of Soviet warheads to American land-based missiles just as great as it is today. And depending on how the two sides decided to configure their force within these limits, the ratio would conceivably move further in the Soviet Union's favour.

The arguments marshalled to defend this aspect of START are not convincing. The first is that the 'window of opportunity' for the Russians claimed by SALT 2's critics was found on reflection to be not as wide or as full of opportunity as was first suggested. If so, then the failure to ratify SALT 2 is at best a reflection of trivial party politics and electioneering and at worst a potentially serious indictment of the American administration's initial frivolity in its approach to arms control.

In order to counter the charge that the ratio of Soviet warheads to aim points has not improved under the START proposals, it has been suggested that the purpose of the American offer was rather (1) to increase the proportion of Soviet warheads needed for a successful first strike on American ICBMs and (2) to render Soviet land-based forces more vulnerable to attack themselves by reducing considerably the number of targets United States forces would have to knock out on the Soviet side. The key to both explanations is the United States MX missile. Once deployed, it is argued, it will be more securely based and will therefore take more Soviet warheads per missile to knock out. And like the new MK 12A warheads on the more vulnerable Minuteman missiles, it will be able, if need be, to knock out Soviet missiles in their silos.

Such is the strategic calculus behind START. But it is scarcely a basis for strategic stability. Mutual vulnerability of population centres has long been seen as a stabilising element and a basic premise of deterrence against the unleashing of nuclear war. Mutual vulnerability of both sides' missile forces to attack, combined with the acquisition by both sides of a clear counterforce (and possible first strike) potential, puts these already destabilising weapons on a hair trigger. In time of crisis the additional uncertainties built into the strategic equation would be enormous.

One idea put forward to counter the problems of vulnerability and particularly American ICBM vulnerability is the reactivation of some sort of ABM defence. The argument runs as follows: if America's land-based forces were secure under the protection of an ABM system, then the relatively greater number of accurate Soviet land-based missiles would cease to be such a problem. That brings the ABM argument back full circle to the position in the early 1970s, when both sides agreed to forego extensive ABM defence precisely because it threatened to undermine security, not reinforce stability. Seen from the Soviet Union, a secure American land-based missile force would pose a very great threat, with the temptation to launch a first strike on Soviet forces all the greater. The result would be the counterdeployment of an equivalent Soviet ABM system. The net gain in terms of security would at best be zero.

Thus, although START has taken some steps in the right direction the problems it does not address – technology, the increasing capacity to knock out enemy missiles and the window of opportunity – will quite possibly build up pressure for unilateral solutions which will ultimately undermine the basic principles of sensible arms control mentioned above. The longer the negotiations last, the greater that danger will be. And unless the American approach to START can accommodate the Soviet Union's legitimate security concerns – not just look for cuts in the Soviet arsenal to enhance American security – then the negotiations will get nowhere. But at this stage the START proposals are just that: proposals. Any final judgement must await progress in the talks themselves and a final agreement.

NUCLEAR-FREE NONSENSE

Another proposal for avoiding nuclear war is the creation of nuclear free zones, particularly in Europe. At first glance the argument may seem a compelling one. There is every good reason to prevent the spread of nuclear weapons to parts of the world where they do no now exist. Where they do already exist, the issue is more complex. Some of the difficulties involved have already been outlined above in the argument against unilateral disarmament and in drawing the distinction in practice between the premises of the 'disarmers' and those of the arms controllers. The problem of security and nuclear weapons in Europe is examined at length in the next chapter. However, since the creation of nuclear-free zones has long been part of the debate on arms control, the argument should be addressed here too. One point has to be made clear: although geographically it is possible to draw lines around nuclear-free zones and ban the emplacement of weapons there, it is not possible to safeguard any such zones from the use of nuclear weapons from outside. Nuclear-free zones can be created at the stroke of a pen: there is no such thing as a nuclear-safe zone. The call for nuclear-free zones ignores technology and concentrates on geography. But geography is largely irrelevant in the nuclear age.

The argument that removal of nuclear weapons from Europe would insulate Europe from superpower conflict is patently absurd. And the argument that weapons drive conflict not vice versa is, as already suggested, one worthy of the ostrich. An arms race can gain a momentum of its own and lead to war, as happened before the First World War, but only when first unleashed by the conflicting interests of the states concerned. Even without nuclear weapons on their soil, the democracies of Western Europe would still be a political and ideological threat to the Soviet Union – and a major prize to be denied to the other side in the event of superpower conflict. Neutrality is no more an option for Western Europe than it has been for Eastern Europe. Without the ability to defend itself in the nuclear age, Western Europe would by its own volition be wide open to nuclear blackmail. However, a Western Europe capable of defending itself need not have to face the choice between red and dead.

CRITICAL CHOICES FOR ARMS CONTROL

It has been said of the arms control process in the 1970s that it gained a bureaucratic foothold – by the institutionalisation of the SALT talks in American–Soviet relations, the creation of formal negotiating machinery and the almost permanent assignment of government personnel to the SALT process – but that it lost its popular base. Almost by definition the kind of methodical step-by-step approach adopted by arms controllers to the problem of nuclear weapons can never compete with the dramatic, even if empty, gesture or the emotional appeal so characteristic of today's peace movement. Arms control is a complex business; its appeal has to be to intellect and reason, not pure emotion. Can its prospects be improved for the 1980s?

Arms control needs a better press. Gestures, at least of the constructive kind, should not be ruled out. The Soviet Union is well practised at issuing broad appeals for peace, whose purpose is not always in harmony with the genuine security interests of the west. President Reagan's call for a 'zero option' in talks on nuclear weapons in Europe was deliberately pitched in part to shame the Soviet Union to the negotiating table, in part to take some of the wind out of the sails of Europe's anti-nuclear movement (which, unlike its American counterpart, is more fascinated with unilateral disarmament than the harder business of negotiating a more stable nuclear balance). In their more studious moments both superpowers still accept that, short of the – unlikely – capitulation of either side, there is really no substitute for painstaking negotiation. In the end it is governments that have to agree; mass movements cannot sign binding treaties on arms control. At the same time it would do the cause of balanced arms control no harm in the west to have governments demonstrate that the pursuit of peace is not the moral monopoly of the extreme left, just as the will to national defence is not the patriotic monopoly of the extreme right.

A better and more exciting public image for those in the centre, unconvinced by the arguments of the unilateralists or the pursuit of military superiority, would help, but it is not enough. What arms control needs to recover momentum and recapture the moral high ground in the nuclear debate is demonstrable success. Two of the prime objectives of continued arms control negotiations have already been mentioned in the discussion of SALT: a more stable and secure nuclear balance at as low a level as possible; and a rein on technologies that could undermine the strategic balance and impair mutual deterrence.

Although ill-thought-out cuts in weapons can create more problems than they solve, there is no doubt that establishing a balance at a lower threshold – lowering the ceilings already agreed in SALT 1 and SALT 2 – would help to inspire greater public confidence in the commitment of both superpowers to arms control. But the prime purpose of reductions should be to stabilise the balance, not just to lower numbers. Limiting more strictly the numbers of launchers is not enough. SALT 2, whatever its other faults, demonstrated that, by putting an upper limit on the number of permissible MIRVed systems, and hence a rein of sorts on the number of warheads, the increasing Soviet threat to America's land-based strategic weapons could at least be checked, leaving it open to the United States to counter that threat. Further compression of SALT's roomy walls and ceilings can be achieved. Further cuts in both launchers and warheads can be made without incurring the destabilising effects of the Kennan cuts.

This point appears to have been accepted by both superpowers, however bellicose their public statements have become since the breakdown of SALT. President Reagan has based his new American proposals on the need to reduce significantly the numbers of warheads allowed under SALT so far and to put firm and finite limits on their totals. To make his point he has dispensed with the acronym SALT and replaced it with START, strategic arms *reduction* talks. The principle is a sound one. And the impression gained from hints dropped by Soviet spokesmen is that the principle of reductions is now accepted in the Soviet Union too. The task will be to turn agreement on principle into a detailed agreement acceptable to both sides, which will enhance strategic stability.

FIRST STRIKE; SECOND STRIKE

A key indication of the seriousness of the two sides will be the kinds of cuts made or demanded. Within the overall limits set in any new arms control agreement, special efforts need to be made to curb the most dangerous and destabilising weapons, i.e. those designed for offensive, rather than defensive missions. Land-based ICBMs are the main culprits here. Despite advances in other technologies, for the time being they remain the most accurate missiles in both sides' strategic arsenal, capable of hitting precise military targets, including the ICBMs of the other side. Although the Soviet Union's 'heavy' ICBMs have grabbed all the publicity, American Minuteman missiles equipped with a new MK 12A warheads and the new MX missiles will also have a silo-busting capability – the ability to destroy enemy missiles inside their protective silos. As such, ICBMs lend themselves to counterforce missions and, whatever the real intentions of either side, these weapons raise fears of surprise attack. Since deterrence is based on assured second strike capacity, and the possibility of a first strike capability can radically upset the strategic balance, land-based

ICBMs are likely to continue to upset calculations of deterrence, especially in times of tension or crisis.

Because they are primarily counterforce weapons, ICBMs are an obvious category of weapons to limit if the balance is to be made more stable. Concern over the theoretical possibility of a Soviet disarming first strike against America's land-based ICBMs had already increased the pressure there to deploy a mobile missile, MX (although new basing modes are now under review, including the 'dense pack' or close cluster of missiles) or else to deploy many smaller missiles to increase vastly the number of targets the Soviet Union would have to knock out, or to reactivate ABM technology for hard-site missile defence. The last two of these solutions would certainly rupture the ceilings set in SALT 2 (and the first may do so too) and all would complicate enormously the search for progress in arms control. In the meantime the Soviet Union, for its part, is no doubt preparing itself for a need to meet any future technological challenge by making further improvements to its own ICBM force. An American move to break SALT 2 would also reinforce Soviet resistance to a reduction in numbers of ICBMs, particularly its heavy, silo-busting variety. In other words, the cost of deterrence, both in economic and arms control terms, would increase.

The problem of ICBM vulnerability is not an easy one to solve. The search for security against an enemy first strike capacity through improvements, quantitative or qualitative, to existing ICBM deployments automatically brings either side perilously close to developing a first strike capacity of its own. The problem arises because of two developments: the first is the asymmetrical balance of forces in the strategic arsenals of the two superpowers. As already noted, the Soviet Union has a much greater proportion of its forces based on land (although it still has more submarine launchers than the United States), partly for traditional reasons (the primacy of land forces), partly for geographical reasons, partly because it is apparently not yet prepared to put its faith in its less developed submarine (SLBM) technology (see below). And the Soviet Union has long adhered to what can best be called a war-fighting doctrine. Soviet doctrine asserts that the best way to deter the outbreak of nuclear war is to be prepared to fight one and to aim to win it once it has started (which is not the same as aiming to start a war). At the strategic level, land-based ICBMs are the most accurate and most lethal weapons under present conditions and have a crucial role in Soviet strategy.

The second explanation for the problem is the attachment of both sides to traditional basing modes and the practice of measuring national strength and security by counting and comparing numbers of weapons in each category, rather than looking at how the weapons in the different categories further national strategic objectives. The Soviet Union's attachment to its ICBMs and its reluctance to dispense with such weapons in favour of less vulnerable, more stable forces is matched by the American attachment to its strategic triad, each leg of which – land, sea and air – has to remain in place and invulnerable to a disarming first strike for American's nuclear planners to feel secure.

It may well be that for sensible arms control agreements to be concluded in the future neither the American triad, nor the Soviet Union's traditional force structure, can be considered sacred. For example, if the overall aim is enhanced security and if ICBMs are so destabilising and so vulnerable, why not scrap them? The argument is not as daft as it sounds. The main argument for scrapping ICBMs is that by pushing nuclear weapons out to sea or putting them on planes they are no longer sitting targets: their vulnerability is reduced, and their survivability is enhanced. So is their flexibility – they can have more than one role in national strategy. By making them less vulnerable, they acquire a second strike capacity – and they therefore fit better into a strategy of flexible response.

The most obvious argument against scrapping land-based ICBMs, apart from the one that too many bureaucratic hackles would be raised by such a radical departure from tradition, is that the Soviet Union would not buy it. If the purpose of arms control is to enhance security, then the Soviet Union would be unlikely to accept a proposal which cut deeply into the most effective branch of its own nuclear force while allowing the United States to exploit its advantage in submarine technology. The Russians turned down flat the Carter proposals which took a stride in that direction. But since then both sides have thought more seriously about reducing arms as the Soviet response to the Reagan START proposals has demonstrated.

A radical reduction in one subset of nuclear weapons would take more imagination than either of the two superpowers has shown so far. On the other hand, the arms control process has been in part a learning process on both sides. If START is to do a serious job of arms control, pressure needs to be kept on both superpowers to control more effectively the most destabilising weapons in the strategic balance. Indeed the Soviet Union is aware that its land-based missiles will become increasingly vulnerable to attack as this decade wears on. What it still lacks in numbers of SLBM warheads, and submarine technology, it has already made up in number of SLBM launchers (576 for the United States; 950 for the Soviet Union). If the Soviet Union can be persuaded that its own force posture is not set in stone, and that its security can be better guaranteed by a different force structure, that at least is a sensible direction to work in. And since both sides insist they are not aiming at a first strike capability, let them put intelligent arms control where their mouth is.

If the Soviet Union cannot be persuaded to accept a bilateral renunciation of land-based ICBMs – and the chances are that it cannot for the present – the issue of ICBM vulnerability will continue to vex the United States, with its smaller land-based ICBM force. Rather than opting for a greater proliferation of ICBMs or a return to destabilising ABM technology, why not simply remove the targets? What is needed is not a more secure first strike force but a more reliable second strike force. Seen as part of a future rethink of America's entire nuclear force posture, the unilateral scrapping of American ICBMs would not amount to a unilateral concession to the Soviet Union. On the contrary:

1. it would end the dilemma over ICBM vulnerability and its dangerous and destabilising implications, especially in times of tension;
2. by putting more of its strategic forces out to sea, the United States would gain flexibility without jettisoning deterrence;
3. with expected advances in SLBM technology – including the advanced Trident submarine programme now well under way – this would enhance rather than impair America's war-fighting capability;
4. it would put a large dent in Soviet assumptions about the continuing utility of its own heavy missiles and targeting philosophy;
5. it would deprive the Soviet Union of the psychological advantage that even a theoretical first strike capability against America's ICBMs now gives it (whether in its own mind or that of the United States);
6. if the Soviet Union still refused categorically to cooperate it would be open to the charge of perpetuating the instability in the strategic balance which such first strike weapons have caused;
7. if part of a balanced reappraisal of strategic parity, it could encourage the Soviet Union to move more quickly towards scaling down its own huge ICBM force and the development of technologies more clearly suited for an assured *second* strike.

The idea of scrapping land-based ICBMs is not new. Yet the implications of such a move have not been properly thought through. There are those who insist, on purely numerical terms, that three classes of strategic forces must always be better than two. Submarines are also more costly to build and deploy than land-based missiles in fixed silos. But 'cost-effectiveness' must also take into account the impact of different forces on the stability of the strategic balance. However, these are not the only arguments against scrapping ICBMs.

So far at least, submarine-launched missiles cannot be delivered onto their targets as accurately as land-based missiles. Communications with submarines are more vulnerable to disruption than communications on land. And there is always the fear that a breakthrough in anti-submarine warfare (ASW) will make the seas transparent and render submarines quickly vulnerable to enemy attack.

These are real problems but they are not insurmountable. The balance of accuracy advantage in favour of land-based missiles is changing. ASW is a problem. But a proposal of this kind needs to be protected by an arms control package which included limits on ASW and any other technological developments likely to undermine arms control and the preservation of a secure second strike capability by either side (see below).

The problem is even trickier for the Soviet Union. Not only does its submarine technology lag behind that of the United States (although it is now rapidly MIRVing its submarine-launched missiles), but also for geographic reasons its fleet is more constrained in its operations. There are a limited number of choke points through which submarines attached to the various Soviet fleets must pass to gain access to strategically important expanses of ocean. In theory it should therefore be easier to keep tabs on their movements. For these and other reasons, including the reflex argument of tradition on the Soviet side too, the Soviet Union will probably not be prepared suddenly to dispense with its land-based forces. However it should none the less remain a principle behind the American approach to arms control to encourage the Soviet Union as far as possible in that direction and to seek out ways of limiting Soviet missile forces while preserving Soviet security and an assured second strike capacity.

However, it should be remembered that submarine-launched missiles present their own problems for arms control. A particular concern for the Soviet Union is the enhanced accuracy of the missiles to be deployed under the American Trident submarine programme. Although SLBMs are valuable second strike weapons, the higher accuracy of Trident missiles gives them at least the potential to launch a surprise attack with the ability to knock out precise military targets in the Soviet Union, including some Soviet land-based missiles. The threat is real and the Soviet Union can be expected to push hard for clear limits on SLBMs under any new arms control package. Paradoxically the Trident factor could also encourage the Soviet Union to push ahead with its own submarine technology and switch its focus away from its land-based monster missiles that have upset arms control talks in the past. If handled properly in the START talks, SLBMs could bring more stability to the nuclear balance and so enhance the security of *both* sides.

TECHNOLOGY NEEDS CONTROLLING TOO

Several threads in the technology tangle have already been picked up in the discussion so far. They include the potentially destabilising effects of defensive technologies, such as ABM, which can undermine the principal of mutual deterrence; anti-submarine warfare, which can undermine efforts to move towards a more stable balance based on assured second strike capabilities (and because ASW overlaps with conventional warfare, it would be hard to negotiate as a package); new refinements in warhead technology that give either side's counterforce weapons the disturbing ability to 'disarm' the opponent's land-based weapons at a single blow; and a whole host of new technologies which could conceivably undermine current verification procedures and so make effective monitoring of arms control agreements impossible. In short, the possibilities for undermining arms control by means of technological 'progress' are enormous. Thus sensible arms control must include parallel efforts to negotiate limits on the technology race.

Technological developments have raised one worry in particular: how to safeguard command, control and communications networks so that if ever a disaster did occur and nuclear weapons were ever exchanged, not only would national commanders be able to keep track of their own nuclear forces, but also the political leaderships of both sides could reserve to themselves the critical decisions of escalation, de-escalation and bargaining to bring the crisis to an end. It is for this reason that anti-satellite weapons (ASAT) under development by both sides have begun to cause considerable alarm. This 'star wars' technology is, relatively speaking, still in its infancy, although it has been on the drawing boards of scientists since the 1950s – even before the first Sputnik was launched in 1957.

The United States and the Soviet Union have so far been successful in banning the bomb in outer space. Military activities in space were partially restricted by the 1967 outer space treaty, in which the signatories agreed not to station nuclear weapons or weapons of mass destruction in orbit or on celestial bodies. Nuclear tests in outer space are also banned, as are military bases. SALT 2 reinforced these restrictions by prohibiting the development, testing and deployment of systems to put weapons into orbit. But SALT does not cover ASAT.

ASAT technology could take any of several forms. And its prime purpose would be to destroy the communications satellites of the other side. Killer satellites, capable of tracking down and then colliding with other satellites in space were one of its earliest forms. In recent years research has focused on the use of satellite-mounted lasers or else more cumbersome particle beam weapons to explode or disable enemy satellites. Neither technology has yet been fully developed; both are complex and beyond the scope of this book to examine in detail. However, the basic principles behind ASAT technology are easy enough to grasp – and the dangers for arms control and the maintenance of strategic parity are clear.

Satellites are vital for communications and reconnaisance – not to mention verification of existing arms control agreements. Both the Soviet Union and the United States rely on satellites, but they are especially vital to the United States which cannot fall back so easily on land communications, since its major allies and part of its forces are an ocean or more away. Should either side develop a fully operational and effective ASAT system, able to sweep the skies clear of satellites of all opposing powers, it would gain overwhelming strategic advantage.

Of course, satellites can not only be attacked, they can also be defended. The satellites in orbit today are all relatively vulnerable to attack, since emphasis has been on packing them with as much working equipment at possible. Satellite skins can be hardened to withstand ASAT attack; jamming techniques and other forms of interference can be employed to confuse a killer satellite before it has a chance to attack its target. Yet the costs of defence against ASAT would be enormous and the payload on satellites greatly reduced as a consequence.

The development of lasers for use in space is particularly worrying for another reason: lasers also have application in ABM research. The

1972 ABM treaty specifically prohibited the development, testing and deployment of 'ABM systems or components which are . . . space based'. A successfully developed satellite-based laser weapon could conceivably be used defensively to shoot down incoming enemy missiles. But if such a weapon were ever deployed it would also shoot the legs out from under the principle of stability through deterrence. Unlike an ABM system constructed for hard-site missile defence, a space-based ABM would by its nature be able to protect not only missiles, but also cities from enemy attack. Any state with the ability to protect its own weapons and population centres from attack could launch a first strike at enemy targets with impunity.

Such a space-based ABM would have its own problems. It would need to strike at enemy missiles within the space of time of their limited boost phase, and before the separate warheads divided off. Such a system could probably be easily overwhelmed. However submarine-launched missiles would present far easier targets to be picked off. Submarines can only fire one missile at a time, with longer intervals between firings. As a consequence it is again the other side's second strike weapons which are made most vulnerable by such defensive weapons.

Clearly if an ASAT race began in earnest, the two sides could easily provoke each other into pouring billions of dollars in ASAT research and development and in the process only undermine further their own security. Neither side has yet developed a fully operational system. Both are, however, poised to begin more intensive research and development. It was in recognition of both the financial problems and the arms control implications of ASAT that American and Soviet negotiators began talks on the subject in June 1978. The Soviet Union voluntarily suspended ASAT tests while the negotiations were in progress. They had not got very far when, like the SALT talks, they were broken off following the Soviet invasion of Afghanistan in December 1979. The Soviet Union resumed ASAT testing in April 1980. The same problems which brought the negotiators to the table in 1978 persist today. They can only get worse. Unless a decision is made soon to resume ASAT talks, the chance to cap this potentially disastrous star wars technology race may be entirely lost.

What can be done? A simple attempt to ban all ASAT weapons and their components is not enough. Many components of ASAT systems are used in other space programmes. The American space shuttle, for example, has wide military application. What is needed – and probably easier to negotiate and verify – is agreement similar to that contained in the 1972 ABM treaty, namely to ban the testing, deployment or use of any weapons in a manner appropriate for attacking satellites. The idea would be to stunt the growth of offensive ASAT technologies, while allowing research to continue in the search for less destabilising defensive technologies, including satellite protection. The two prime obligations would be to agree not to use, deploy or test (in space) any weapon or system for damaging or destroying satellites, and to agree not to interfere with the functioning of the other side's satellites. Without extensive testing, no ASAT system could be deployed effectively. The alternative would be an ASAT race which would produce no net gain in security for either side and could on the contrary make the strategic balance frighteningly less stable than it is today.

BUILDING CONFIDENCE IN ARMS CONTROL

Aside from agreements specifically to limit weapons or curb destabilising technologies, there is still plenty of room for less dramatic steps to be taken to make the strategic balance more secure and the military threat for either side more predictable and therefore more manageable.

The earliest such step was the establishment of the 'hot line' to facilitate more direct communication between the United States and the Soviet Union in times of crisis. In 1971 the hot line was upgraded by mutual agreement. The same year an Agreement on Measures to Reduce the Risks of Outbreak of Nuclear War, known for short as the 'accidents agreement' was signed. It provided for (1) safeguards against accidental or unauthorised use of nuclear weapons, (2) immediate notification of any accident with nuclear weapons, and (3) advanced notice of planned missile launches beyond national territory and in the direction of the other party. In 1972 an Agreement on the Prevention of Incidents On and Over the High Seas was added to the list.

All these agreements in their own way were designed to reduce the risk of accidental or unintentional conflict. The SALT process itself helped build confidence in the arms control process between the two superpowers in several ways: by establishing the numbers of weapons on either side, by developing agreed monitoring procedures, and by setting up machinery for dealing with charges of infringement of agreed provisions and limits under SALT.

More could be done by both sides to make available information about weapons programmes to prevent the kinds of scares seen in the past, from the 'missile gap' of the late 1950s to the 'window of opportunity' in the 1970s. Proposals have been put forward for the setting up of a permanently staffed joint crisis centre to deal with any unexpected, unintentional developments which could bring the two sides close to nuclear confrontation. And there could be greater willingness by both sides, but particularly by the Soviet Union, to allow the kind of random on-site inspections that could give verification of arms control a better name.

WHERE TO FROM HERE?

Arms control has a future. The discussion in this chapter has focused not on what the precise details of future arms control agreements should be, but rather on the underlying principles that should guide the arms control process. These include:

1. Strict limits on counterforce weapons which encourage fears of surprise attack, and emphasis instead on the development of secure second strike capabilities by both sides. Progress towards this end will undoubtedly be complicated by the different force structures on each side. The Soviet Union has concentrated on building up its land-based forces – the biggest culprits here – to the point where they could theoretically pose a serious threat to the entire American land-based force. The result has been to prod the United States into actions which may in the end produce an even less stable balance than exists today. Once new American submarines and their more accurate warheads are in service they will pose a substantial threat to Soviet land-based missiles.

   That point has begun to sink home. The Soviet Union appears to be ready now to discuss more radical arms control measures than it was prepared to contemplate under SALT 2. At the Geneva START talks, the United States and the Soviet Union need to put forward constructive ideas on how this problem can be resolved without prejudice to the principle of equal security. If the arms spiral is to be cut short, flexibility will be required of both sides. Both must accept that existing force structures will probably have to be modified if a solution is to be found. By the nature of its deployments, the Soviet Union is the worst offender. It should be prepared to acknowledge the genuine security concerns of the United States and work towards the creation of a less offensive, less destabilising force posture.

This might mean moving away from the principle, enshrined in SALT 2, of rigidly equal ceilings. Instead of simply counting weapons in the different categories and matching them, more flexible agreements could look at the kinds of missions weapons are designed to accomplish.

2. The move to acquire a secure second strike capability makes little sense if technological breakthroughs threaten to render the greater proportion of such a second strike force vulnerable to direct attack. Second strike weapons are no less lethal than first strike weapons. It bears repeating – the new Trident missiles will come close to matching some of the accuracy of their land-based counterparts and will cause considerable problems for arms control as a consequence. Their advantage is that they can be withheld from initial use, so that they enhance the deterrence effect. And their relative invulnerability to initial enemy surprise attack removes the frightening 'hair trigger' mechanism which adds so greatly to tension and uncertainty in times of crisis.

3. Command, control and communications links have to be secured as far as possible from disruption both in peacetime and in wartime. In peacetime, secure communications and reconnaisance add to confidence that arms control agreements already signed are being successfully monitored and verified. In time of conflict the ability to maintain political control, particularly over the use of nuclear weapons, would be crucial in bringing any conflict to a rapid conclusion. For both these reasons talks are urgently needed on limiting new technologies which threaten communications links and particularly satellite communications.

4. Not only offensive, but also defensive weapons can upset the strategic balance and offer one side or the other considerable unilateral advantage. Any attempt to make use of such an advantage would have disastrous repercussions on the future prospects for intelligent arms control. The ABM treaty of 1972 should, therefore, stand and where necessary be strengthened to remove any doubts about its efficacy.

5. Both sides could contribute far more than they have done to the building of mutual confidence in the process of arms control. The provision of more information on national programmes would help strengthen the verification of arms control agreements already in

place. It would also help prevent the kinds of scares which, although later proved to be unfounded, can have serious repercussions on the arms spiral. The Soviet Union in particular has a serious case to answer here. Its obsession with secrecy has proved highly detrimental to arms control and the building of confidence in verification procedures. Greater confidence in verification procedures would help the arms control process move along more quickly and imaginatively.

6. Finally, but most important, there needs to be a greater readiness to accommodate the legitimate security concerns of both sides if a stable balance is to be achieved.

All steps are manageable given political will on both sides. Taken together or taken separately they will not remove entirely the dangers posed by the existence of nuclear weapons or the threat of nuclear war. But unless the two superpowers can show progress in controlling effectively and reducing their own nuclear stockpiles, they can have little hope of persuading other states to forego acquisition of nuclear weapons too. Unfortunately, in the past the big powers have often proved themselves to be just as small-minded as some of the smaller powers in taking the initiative on arms control. They need to be prodded constantly. Utopian arguments of 'world disarmament' will have less effect on them than realistic and constructive new ideas on arms control.

At the same time the problems facing genuine arms control efforts should not be underestimated. However much goodwill can be generated on either side, some of the problems may prove insoluble. And since arms control agreements must stand up in the bad times just as well as in the good, progress will always seem slower than most people would like. Nuclear weapons will not suddenly disappear at the stroke of a pen. The easy slogans of world disarmament and banning the bomb cannot substitute for the infinitely more complicated and less popular task of controlling the development, production, testing and deployment of nuclear weapons.

Security is best enhanced by binding agreements on arms control. Yet the nuclear weapons powers should not allow themselves to be mesmerised by the process and so lose sight of the goal. Unilateral steps, for example modifications of force structures, should not be ruled out where they can enhance security and help speed up progress towards the achievement of stable deterrence with minimum force.

This is not time for despair. Arms control has come a long way already. SALT 1 and SALT 2 were long in preparation and far from perfect agreements, yet they did succeed in laying solid groundwork for future progress. They were necessary steps on the way. Both superpowers have accepted in principle that the next stage must involve more radical cuts in their strategic arsenals. Where one cut has been made, and seen not to upset the strategic balance, others can follow. The upward spiral of nuclear weapons acquisition of the past thirty years can be reversed.

That task would be considerably easier if arms control talks could proceed within a relatively stable environment. That means an acceptance on the part of political leaders, both in the United States and in the Soviet Union, that arms control talks have a very considerable and long-term strategic value, not just a short-term political purpose.

In the nuclear age, while the political, economic and military hostility between east and west endures, peace cannot be secured for the west without weapons. But nor can peace be secured solely through weapons either. Since nuclear weapons cannot simply be cursed out of existence, the most effective way of making sure that the underlying conflicts between east and west do not spill over into armed conflicts is to use arms control to achieve a more stable balance of forces at the lowest possible level.

3 Europe between the Superpowers

LAWRENCE FREEDMAN

Two features of the post-1945 world are striking when put in the context of the history of international politics. First, the two largest powers have been deeply antagonistic towards each other and as a result have accumulated massive armed might – yet their forces have never clashed directly. Second, there have been many wars throughout the globe except on the continent which remains the focal point of great power conflict and which has the bloodiest history of all – Europe.

The reason is not hard to find. The biographies, public utterances of the leaders of both east and west and, most importantly, their actions in the most severe crises attest to their fear of nuclear war. In a perverse way this unprecedented destructive power has brought an equally unprecedented degree of caution and circumspection in the management of relations between the major powers.

It is of course difficult to prove a negative. One cannot be sure that another war would have broken out in Europe if these nuclear weapons did not exist, but there is some common ground among all those involved in the current debate that in important ways the prospect of nuclear war has terrorised us all into a more peaceable existence than might otherwise have been the case.

The question is 'for how long will this continue?' After all, there was widespread revulsion at the thought of another war in 1918, at the end of the First World War, yet twenty years later the same powers were fighting again. There was a general expectation in the 1930s that a future war would see centres of civilisation pounded into rubble. This did not serve as a deterrent and air raids became a feature of the Second World War. In an international system in which conflict is endemic, the risk of something terrible happening can never be removed. Yet it remains the case that despite the mistrust and hostility between the nuclear powers they have been so wary of the dangers of full-scale war that they have avoided any armed clashes let alone nuclear exchanges. The only exception has been some border skirmishes between the Russians and the Chinese.

The answer to the question of how long we can go on before nuclear weapons will be used in anger again cannot be answered by means of some theoretical model of the international system or in the statistics of probabilities. It is to be found in an analysis of the actual political and military relations between the nuclear powers. Such an analysis should be able to identify the risks of a breakdown in these relations and point to what must be done to reduce these risks.

For Europeans this analysis is inevitably dominated by the roles played by the superpowers in the affairs of the continent and, in particular, in their responsibility for the deep division of the continent into NATO and the Warsaw Pact. Behind much of the current anti-nuclear campaigns is a resentment at this division and a pessimism that, as the instruments of their respective superpowers, these alliances are being used to sustain a new arms race which will eventually bring Europe to disaster. It is conceded that nuclear deterrence may have been a stabilising influence in the past but now, it is feared, deterrence is breaking down, and we face nuclear holocaust. In this chapter I will consider the analysis upon which this gloomy judgement is based.

THE CASE FOR THE PROSECUTION

From the publications of groups such as the campaign for European Nuclear Disarmament (END) the following set of arguments can be gleaned. Explicitly they reject the NATO preoccupation with a Soviet 'threat'. The assumption is that the Kremlin has its hands full coping with Eastern Europe so that it no longer has either the time or inclination to pursue aggressive designs on Europe. It is now the United States which is seen to be the more reckless of the super-powers.

This image is a result of the Reagan administration's belligerent rhetoric in foreign policy, and occasional actions to match, combined with perceived changes in strategic doctrine. It is argued that the United States is now shaping up for a great confrontation with the USSR, with the trigger probably to be found in some Third World trouble-spot. Wherever it starts, the confrontation will soon be visited on Europe because that is where the military alliances of the super-powers are organised and prepared for battle.

Even more disturbing than the thought that Europe may find itself engulfed in a war because of some global irresponsibility of the United States in pursuit of its own unique and misguided objectives, is the thought that the United States intends to fight this war with nuclear weapons in the expectation that the dreadful effects of such a conflict could be confined to the continent and need barely incon-venience North America. The evidence for this is to be found in doctrines of 'limited nuclear war' and the weapons that are being introduced into Europe to implement this doctrine – Tomahawk cruise missiles and Pershing ballistic missiles. Europe will serve only as host to these missiles and will have no control over their use.

The fact that the governments of Western Europe have connived at and even justified this state of affairs demonstrates just how ensnared they have been by cold war propaganda and their supineness in the face of American power. They seek to cover themselves by talking hopefully of arms control, despite the patent failure of the relevant negotiations to achieve anything of consequence and the hypocrisy and cynicism with which they have been conducted. The only remedy is to detach Western Europe from the United States, expelling the latter's military hardware and personnel, in order to reorganise sec-urity policy on a less provocative basis around concepts of territorial defence. In doing so, Soviet hegemony over Eastern Europe would be undermined dramatically for it has been legitimised on the basis of the 'NATO threat'. The Soviet satellites could seize greater auton-omy and re-establish their historical links with Western Europe. A Europe could then be created free of the malign influences of both nuclear weapons and superpowers.

This statement may be oversimplified and oversystematic but it does bring together the sort of ideas that are found in the anti-nuclear movement. A substantial amount is read into the plans for the basing of US nuclear weapons in Europe. The implication behind much of the campaigning is that if these plans could only be reversed then not only will a desperately dark future be averted but a bright future made possible.

So at the centre of the debate is the role of US nuclear forces based in Europe. On whether or not these forces are believed to reinforce security by deterring aggression or alternatively to degrade security by introducing an avoidable risk of devastation, much else depends.

The argument that will be developed in this chapter is that there is no reason to believe that the strategic conditions that have brought a form of peace to Europe are about to collapse. If there is a risk it is in a breakdown of political relations rather than of military relations. If there is discomfort with the current strategic position then the West Europeans have only themselves to blame, for it is largely a product of their wishes and previous perceptions of interest. They are not the victims of some superpower ploy. Indeed, analysis of NATO's proposed programme of theatre nuclear force modernisation suggests that it increases the risk to the United States more than to Europe. There is a case to be made for reducing NATO's dependence on nuclear weapons, but not for either dismantling the alliance or abandoning all means of nuclear deterrence. Even when making this case it is important not to ignore the different costs and risks involved in a major shift in policy.

Because so much of the current argument depends on assumptions concerning the motives behind past policy and plans, much of this chapter will consist of an account of the manner by which NATO arrived at its current strategic doctrine. In doing so it is hoped to illuminate arguments that are sometimes forgotten but remain valid for the current debate. Since the impression is now that it is the United States which is pushing for a predominantly nuclear strategy while Europeans wish to put greater stress on conventional forces, it is particularly important to remember that until quite recently it was presumed that the positions were the reverse. It is West European governments who have been the most insistent over the past two decades on NATO's nuclear emphasis and the maintenance of US nuclear bases on European soil. Before we wonder how our representatives could indulge in such folly, we must examine the assumptions as to the nature of the strategic environment and Europe's interests within it which lay behind this insistence on the primacy of nuclear deterrence. It may be that the time has come to move beyond these assumptions but in doing so it is important to recognise that they were not necessarily so frivolous or misguided that they can be readily dismissed.

THE AMERICAN COMMITMENT

When the alliance was first put together the main benefit to Europe was seen to rest not so much in access to the military might of the

United States, including its atomic arsenal, but in the actual commitment of the United States to come to the aid of the western democracies in any future war. In the two world wars of the twentieth
century the entrance of the United States had been delayed. This
meant that its eventual allies had to take a battering before relief
came and took effect. It was believed that if either the Kaiser or the
Führer had known that the enormous power of the United States was
going to be brought to bear in the coming conflict they would have
thought longer and harder before embarking on aggression. Their
calculations of cost and risk would have looked very different.

The hope in 1949 was therefore that any Soviet leader need not
suffer from the illusion that the traditional American reluctance to
involve itself in European squabbles would overcome its natural
sympathy for its fellow democracies. A treaty that made it clear that
an attack on one would be viewed as an attack on all was expected to
serve this purpose. From the American viewpoint this commitment
could be justified by the proposition that if by some mischance the
Eurasian landmass came to be dominated by a single, hostile power
then a clash that had been put off when the battle for Europe was still
underway would have to be faced under much less propitious conditions. Supporting this proposition was the thought that for the United
States any war in Europe would be limited. Its own territory and
civilians were unlikely to be harmed at all and certainly not invaded.
While its distance from the likely arena of conflict meant that its
involvement need be no more than a matter of choice, as an invasion
was not going to force war upon it, it also meant that the effects of the
fighting could be contained. Moreover, while it still enjoyed a
superiority, if not quite a monopoly, in the new and fearful atomic
bombs then it was highly unlikely that the USSR was going to pick a
fight.

This confidence and optimism was soon overtaken by events. By
the early 1950s the United States had to contemplate their vulnerability to small-scale but quite horrific nuclear attacks by Soviet aircraft on desperate one-way missions. Towards the end of that decade
this sense of vulnerability had increased dramatically. The turning-
point came in the autumn of 1957 when the USSR announced that it
had tested the first intercontinental ballistic missiles and then followed this up by demonstrating its mastery of the relevant technology
with the launching of the world's first artificial earth satellite, Sputnik
1. The oceans could no longer protect the people of the United States.
In a future war they would be as much at risk as the peoples of
Europe. The liability was no longer limited and the unavoidable ques-

tion was posed: would an American President be prepared to put New York, Chicago or Boston at risk for the sake of Paris, London, Bonn or, most likely of all, West Berlin?

The stretches of ocean that no longer protected the US from the ravages of war still protected it, to a large extent, from direct invasion. Its immediate stakes in any conflict were inevitably less than those countries which faced occupation. All this inevitably raised doubts as to the credibility of any US guarantee to Western Europe. The USSR might calculate that, whatever the treaty language, the US would stay out of any European conflict rather than accept a risk of nuclear war.

These doubts were reinforced by the extent to which the United States had encouraged NATO in 1954 to adopt a strategy, known as 'massive retaliation', which largely depended on a presumption of US nuclear superiority. According to this doctrine, an aggressor should not assume that he would be able to shape the character of a war, in either location or types of weapons, to suit his own convenience. The USSR might feel that it could achieve its objectives using only conventional forces, in which it enjoyed superiority, but it should not assume that such a limitation would be observed by NATO. Any attempt to grab a part of the 'free world' could result in massive nuclear retaliation. NATO had come to rely on a US threat to widen dramatically the scope and intensity of any conflict, yet, as critics had pointed out from the start, this threat diminished in credibility as the counter-threat posed by the Soviet nuclear arsenal grew.

As it dawned upon NATO strategists that the developing stalemate in the strategic nuclear relationship between the superpowers might undermine deterrence a number of alternative approaches were considered. Some of these alternative approaches were based on nuclear weapons and they will be considered fully below. For the moment we will be concerned with the question of why the alternative which to many seemed the most obvious was not adopted – the development of conventional forces sufficient to block any Warsaw Pact invasion so that it would not be necessary to consider escalation to the nuclear level.

THE CONVENTIONAL ALTERNATIVE

The logic of the conventional alternative had been recognised as soon as it became evident that the USSR had tested its first atomic bomb in 1949. In 1950 the Truman administration argued that the remaining years of nuclear superiority, which it hoped to extend with the development of the hydrogen bomb, should be used to build up the alliance's conventional forces to the point where there was no need to depend so much on nuclear weapons. In this argument the administration was fortified by the alarm generated in Europe by the North Korean attack on the South, which many believed to be a prelude to or even a decoy for a Soviet attack on Western Europe. In these circumstances there was support for measures that would have been considered politically unthinkable the previous year, such as the rearmament of West Germany and the establishment of a permanent and substantial garrison of US troops in Europe. In 1952 NATO adopted at Lisbon a set of force goals that would have allowed it to match the conventional forces of the USSR and its allies.

This effort was abandoned remarkably quickly, superseded by the new doctrine of massive retaliation. The timing of the change is explained simply by the return of a Republican administration in Washington, and its nature by the views of prominent members of that administration, particularly John Foster Dulles. Only in the assumption that NATO strategy could be based on a US nuclear superiority, which it was prepared and determined to exploit, do these views now seem dated. The other arguments deployed in favour of a nuclear rather than a conventional strategy can be applied to today's circumstances as much as those of the mid-1950s and provide the core of the case that must be answered by those who oppose the nuclear bias in NATO's current strategy.

The most compelling complaint against a conventional strategy was that of cost. The quantum leap in destructive power made possible by nuclear weapons does not require a quantum leap in expenditure. The cost of maintaining properly equipped conventional forces that can be expected to be at the right place at the right time is far greater than that of preparing to devastate the enemy's main political and economic centres with nuclear weapons. The inflationary effects of the rearmament programmes of the 1950s convinced many that the requisite conventional capabilities could only come at the risk of severe economic damage. Such damage would then make it impossible to sustain these capabilities over the long term. In the desire to avoid the choice between 'security and solvency', the comparative cheapness of a nuclear strategy was an attractive feature.

The second argument grew out of the actual experience of fighting a conventional war in Korea. Not only did this serve as a reminder of the horrors of conventional warfare, but it also warned of the frustration and domestic unpopularity of a military stalemate, especially when it was known that this was a result of political constraints which precluded the use of the most powerful weapons available or of the taking of the war into Chinese or Soviet territory. Part of the impulse behind the strategy of 'massive retaliation' was the determination of hard-liners that such constraints would never again apply. A hint of this determination probably did help to sort out the armistice between North and South Korea in 1953, and so gave Dulles the confidence to proclaim a new strategy. The temporary nature of this US confidence, prior to the maturing of the Soviet arsenal, was illuminated by the fact that a decade later the Americans found themselves fighting a war with similar political constraints in Vietnam.

THE LESSONS OF VIETNAM

Vietnam in some ways was a product of the critique of 'massive retaliation' that developed during the second half of the 1950s and was adopted by the Kennedy administration in 1961. The critics had argued that if the US allowed itself to be so dependent on nuclear threats to maintain international order then, as the implementation of these threats appeared to become more and more suicidal, their value would diminish. Eventually all that could be deterred by nuclear threats would be another's nuclear attack. Unless there were means of dealing with lesser threats on their own terms, with each limited conventional challenge the choice would be between, to quote the slogans of the day, 'suicide and surrender' or 'humiliation and holocaust'. The solution was therefore to develop conventional capabilities to deal with a wide range of contingencies. As good Keynesians, Kennedy's advisers did not believe the necessary effort need overburden the economy and the result would provide a great deal of diplomatic flexibility of manoeuvre.

Perhaps the problem was that, by comparison with nuclear warfare, any use of conventional forces appeared low-risk. Maybe, too, having made so much of the benefits of flexible conventional forces there was a desire to demonstrate their virtue in practice, to the detriment of a cool and considered political appreciation. At any rate the American involvement in Vietnam, which grew under Kennedy though it only became a major commitment after 1965, demonstrated that 'limitation' is a very relative concept in these circumstances. Conventional war fought a long way from home turned out to be something that it was easy to enter but difficult to leave, frustrating and unpleasant to fight, deeply unpopular at home and abroad and expensive to sustain, so that even an economy as powerful as that of the United States was faced with the choice of 'guns or butter'.

In some ways the West Europeans anticipated the lessons of Vietnam in objecting to the Kennedy administration's new strategy as it applied to them. Having witnessed grim and violent warfare twice in the twentieth century the Europeans were well aware of the ghastliness of all wars and the difficulties of bringing them to a decisive conclusion. Furthermore, however awkward and costly it was to fight a war overseas, it was infintely worse to serve as the battlefield. The risk was that what might seem limited to the superpowers might be experienced as total by the allies. The fear expressed by West European governments in the early 1960s was that the American desire to reduce the role of its nuclear guarantee to Europe and to stress the potential of renovated and expanded conventional forces was little more than an attempt to reduce the nuclear risk to itself at the expense of increasing the conventional risk to Europe.

Knowing that the US was unlikely to use its nuclear weapons on Europe's behalf, Soviet risk calculations would be simplified enormously. Even if a conventional invasion faltered, the damage to the USSR would be to its pride and reputation, but it could still live to fight another day. The US might then feel proud that aggression had been defeated without great cost to itself. But the people of Europe would be left ravaged and desolate, horrified by the thought of a repeat performance at a later date.

Or suppose that the Soviet invasion prospered some distance before it was halted and a cease-fire agreed. The west as a whole would have limited Soviet gains, but the Federal Republic of Germany would be no more than a barely viable rump. Even if the initial fighting was genuinely limited, unless an agreement could be reached to settle on the status quo ante the government in Bonn would be faced with the choice of having either to concede the loss of territory or, in attempting to push back the invading forces, to accept the devastation of the same territory. Most difficult of all was the outpost of West Berlin, locked inside East Germany, regularly put under pressure by the Warsaw Pact and yet indefensible by conventional means. From this perspective, Western Europe in general, and West Germany in particular, could not but lose in any war however limited it might appear in either Washington or Bonn.

In this suspicion of American intentions, there is some similarity between those views of, by and large conservative, European governments of the early 1960s and the radical protest movement of today. The key difference is that the governments of the 1960s were more absolute and comprehensive in their fears. Limited conventional war was not seen as a relatively soft option but as a recipe for disaster, almost but admittedly not quite as bad as nuclear war itself. The conclusion was that distinctions could not be made between types of warfare or different stages in a process of escalation, but that any war would be so terrible in its consequences, that there was no alternative to deterrence.

Deterrence involved making it clear to the potential enemy that the prospective costs of aggression would far outweigh the prospective gains. He must be in no doubt that a victory which could be recognised as such was out of the question, even if that meant accepting the unavoidability of victory for NATO as well. Deterrence was not served by anything that suggested that the costs of war could be contained within possibly acceptable limits. It was nuclear weapons that made the prospect of war so unthinkable, so that anything which removed these weapons from Soviet calculations helped to make war thinkable. The best course was to stress the likelihood of any conflict 'going nuclear', for even the slightest risk of this prediction turning out to be correct would ensure deterrence. The most foolish course was even to suggest to the USSR that a European adventure need involve only a limited liability, in that the battle could be confined to an area well away from its territory and that the rules of the war would preclude the use of nuclear weapons.

It was certainly the case that European objections to American proposals were based on a greater pessimism as to the possibility of matching Soviet conventional strengths at a tolerable cost, especially given the Warsaw Pact's built-in geographical advantage. The journey for its reserves was less lengthy and hazardous than that for American reserves travelling across the Atlantic. The bright young analysts of the Kennedy and Johnson administrations became convinced that NATO's intelligence estimates had engendered defeatism by exaggerating Warsaw Pact strength. Furthermore the assumption of conventional inferiority when used as a basis for planning turned into a self-fulfilling prophecy. For example, if it was assumed that front-line forces could only hold out for three days, so that in consequence only three days' supply of ammunition was provided, then they certainly would not last more than three days. The case was made that for only modest increases in outlays of men, money and material NATO could put itself in the position where it could cope with the most determined Warsaw Pact attack and so rid itself of dependence on an increasingly incredible US guarantee to use its nuclear arsenal on behalf of its European allies if they were in danger of being overrun in a conventional invasion.

All this seemed so self-evident to the American analysts that they failed to appreciate the anxiety this line of argument engendered in Europe. Apart from the irritation at being lectured to by the smart-aleck college professors, the leaders of Western Europe believed that the United States had lost sight of the political context of the defence debate and the consequences of their theorising for that debate. In truth they doubted whether the USSR was at all interested in attempting to take on NATO. They therefore saw little need to tamper with the current doctrines or force structure, even if they failed to satisfy the exacting requirements of American strategists. They did not think that the US nuclear guarantee had to be 100 per cent credible. As long as the Kremlin could not rule out the possibility of nuclear exchanges with the US, deterrence would be at work. What might upset things was sending the wrong signals to Moscow: that the US itself no longer took its nuclear guarantee to Europe seriously; that it was ready to agree to prevent escalation into the nuclear sphere; that it would fight any European war on the terms the USSR chose to set.

FLEXIBLE RESPONSE

Out of this transatlantic debate came the compromise doctrine of flexible response. It was agreed in 1967, but only after France had withdrawn from NATO's Integrated Military Command. France saw the new US doctrine as an attempt to impose hegemony on Western Europe, by forcing it to accept the risks of association with a rumbustious superpower while denying it the full benefits of US strategic assets. The fact that the Kennedy and Johnson administrations' advocacy of a stronger conventional defence for NATO was combined with a determination to maintain firm control over all nuclear activities, which included discouraging independent nuclear forces in Europe, endeared them even less to Paris. The French concluded that a nuclear deterrent operated by one country could not serve a whole alliance, and therefore decided to build up their own deterrent to serve solely their own national interests, a position that has been upheld by successive French governments with varying degrees of consistency and conviction.

For the rest of the alliance, flexible response involved a reasonable compromise. The Europeans accepted in principle, while doing little about it in practice, that it was advisable to strengthen front-line conventional forces and reserves, and to allot them a greater role in strategic planning. It was accepted that a deterrent that depended on virtually automatic employment of nuclear weapons by the US, before diplomatic and less drastic military options had been fully and visibly exhausted, would not be credible. Moreover, it might need a full-scale conventional clash to raise the passions before nuclear use would be thinkable and also, for that matter, to allow time for the relevant systems to be prepared for use.

In return the Americans accepted that there must be a clear link between their nuclear arsenal and the defence of Europe. The risk of a war 'going nuclear' must be emphasised. To do this it was felt that there should be a likely line of development by which a war could escalate from the first conventional clashes through to all-out nuclear exchanges, should the USSR persist in its aggression. The medium by which the war would be transformed from a conventional clash to one in which nuclear arms would be used would be 'theatre' or 'tactical' nuclear weapons. This peculiar species of weapons could perform this task by being designed to perform traditional military tasks in and around the battlefield. Because of this they bridged the gap between the two types of warfare.

Some of the anti-nuclear literature treats 'flexible response' as a late 1970s phenomenon mainly concerned with flexibility in nuclear forces. In fact for the proponents in the 1960s the flexible options were all conventional. It was only in attempting to convince the USSR of a possible slide into nuclear war that distinct types of nuclear response were postulated. This brings us to the most controversial area of NATO's force structure. The controversy has risen out of confusion over the purpose and value of these weapons. NATO, in a sense, sought to take advantage of this confusion by ensuring that it was shared by the USSR. The confusion itself was of long standing and to appreciate how it had come about we must take another step backwards in time to the debates of the 1950s over 'massive retaliation'.

TACTICAL NUCLEAR WEAPONS

The origins of the concept of tactical nuclear weapons go back to the 1940s. Many of the nuclear scientists who had been responsible for the development of the first atomic bombs were distressed by the persistent concentration on perfecting means of mass destruction. The issue came to a head in late 1949 when the Truman administration decided to develop the hydrogen bomb, which would have unlimited destructive potential. Single bombs could destroy major cities. As an alternative, the liberal group among the nuclear scientists argued for small atomic weapons that could be used as unusually powerful artillery. The leader of this group, Robert Oppenheimer, argued the need to get 'battle back to the battlefield'.

The adjective 'tactical' reflected this aspiration to push nuclear weapon development into directions close to established weapons types rather than into the new and horrific realms of city-busting. Weapons designed for this latter purpose came to be known as 'strategic'. At a time of scarcity in nuclear materials it seemed as if these two types might be in competition. As the technology improved, the age of nuclear plenty arrived, so both types of weapons were produced in profusion.

The new tactical weapons did not displace the purpose-built weapons of mass destruction. They arrived in Europe to join NATO forces in the shape of artillery shells and even mines (atomic demolition mines). This move tended to be approved of by those anxious to find an alternative to strategies dependent on threats of mass destruction, especially as the realisation of these threats would invite an equally destructive retaliation.

The hope was that these weapons could reinforce NATO's position *vis-à-vis* the Warsaw Pact. It was believed that they might uniquely favour NATO. Apart from the expectation that it would be many years before the USSR would have the spare resources to develop its own arsenal, it was suggested that small nuclear weapons might be of greatest value on the battlefield to the defence. As the offence concentrated its forces to prepare an attack it would offer choice targets. All this assumed that tactical nuclear weapons could be used as if they were tactical conventional weapons – without any inhibitions.

By the early 1960s this hope had largely been dashed. It was not only that the USSR had developed its own forces for use in and around a European battlefield, or that their individual size, inaccuracy and propensity to high fall-out mocked Western notions of measured and controlled exchanges. It was not even the analysis which demonstrated that nuclear weapons might favour the offence as much as the defence, being used as traditional artillery to blast holes in the defensive positions. The real difficulty was that it proved impossible to consider the use of tactical nuclear weapons as being more akin to the use of conventional weapons than strategic nuclear weapons.

The problem was revealed in consideration of the practicalities of tactical nuclear warfare. However innocuous the tactical weapons might seem by comparison with 'city-busters', explosive yields approaching those of the weapons that destroyed Hiroshima and Nagasaki were often involved, including the attendant fall-out. Because of their limited range and their likely targets they would in all probability be used over the territory of the defending country. For the population being defended the consequences would be disastrous. Exercises in the mid-1950s suggested that if only NATO weapons were used German casualties could soon reach the millions. When Soviet retaliation was added the prospect became even worse. And if the use of these weapons brought no definite advantage to the attacker or the defender, then the move to the 'higher' stage of strategic exchanges was still likely. All that would have happened was that nuclear weapons would be introduced into the conflict earlier than necessary. Moreover there were no obvious means whereby nuclear use could be contained on a battlefield. Once appropriate targets moved beyond forces at the front line to lines of supply, which were likely to pass through centres of population, then tactical nuclear use would be even less easy to distinguish from strategic nuclear use.

The implications of this line of argument were not lost on politicians, soldiers and the public. A nuclear weapon is a nuclear weapon is a nuclear weapon, and no terminological tricks can turn it into something more modest and tolerable. Whatever the promise of containing the effects in one battle zone, it was evident that the immediate consequences of any employment would be unpalatable for those being defended and that there was still the risk of speedy escalation into something much worse. In practical terms this would mean that early nuclear use would not be authorised, even in the face of a massive Soviet conventional onslaught. Yet if early use was not authorised then, when this option of penultimate resort had to be faced (strategic exchanges being the last resort), the conditions would be even less propitious – with enemy forces more dispersed and further on into friendly territory, and thus closer to the population being defended. And even if use was then authorised the question would remain as to the value of taking such a drastic step when a response in kind by the USSR could negate and possibly supersede any temporary military gains. (In a war of attrition, the larger force still tends to prevail.)

All these problems ensured that at the very least tactical nuclear weapons could not and would not be used as if they were normal weapons. Elaborate procedures of political consultation were established within NATO, agreed in Athens in 1962, which would if nothing else involve substantial delay before the 'go-code' was released. Tight political control was established over the character of any employment, with strict rules relating this employment to whether or not it would take place in friendly territory and proximity to civilian areas. It became clear that, whatever the nomenclature, any use of 'tactical' nuclear weapons would be governed by criteria that were 'strategic' in the true meaning of the term.

It was thus allowed that the confusion in the concept underlying the deployment of these weapons required preparing methods for deciding on employment according to the specific requirements of a conflict. However this begged the question of whether any useful purpose was served at all by deployment of weapons that could not be properly accommodated in any serious battle plans. Why then were these weapons not removed as their inadequacies became so exposed?

It was not that the Kennedy administration was reluctant to remove the thousands of these battlefield nuclear weapons that had been introduced into Europe during the days of the Eisenhower administration. The politics of removing something in being is quite different from that of putting it there in the first place. Most of the European forces had purchased delivery vehicles so as to be able to employ nuclear warheads in battle if handed over from American custody where they were kept under a dual-key arrangement. European governments had put a lot of effort into justifying the introduction of these weapons to the public and felt that they would be made to look foolish if the policy was reversed. Furthermore the USSR was now following suit, so in a sense the element of choice was being removed.

All these were negative reasons. For positive arguments all it was possible to do was draw on the confusion engendered in NATO minds and to translate this into the Soviet mind. Simply by being on

European soil so close to the likely combat zone, it was easier to imagine use of these nuclear weapons being authorised than if they were well out of things, patrolling in the oceans or sitting in silos in the US. There was no logical reason why a decision to use nuclear weapons would be any easier for an American President with one type of weapon rather than another, but intuition suggested that somehow a decision that was shaped by the exigencies of a European conflict might more plausibly 'go nuclear' than one taken from one step removed. At any rate the Kremlin might believe this to be the case and successful deterrence requires no more than that the calculating men of the Kremlin consider the risks to be too high. If some in NATO circles were concerned that these weapons introduced a danger of premature escalation to nuclear exchanges then it would do no harm if similar fears abounded in Moscow.

This fitted in with the European view that the objective of security policy was to demonstrate to the USSR that any conflict would in all probability get out of control and move into horrific destruction. The fact that this destruction would be mutual was not believed to detract necessarily from deterrence because the initial calculation of risk would have to be made by the party undertaking the first act of escalation – invasion. However, it did not accord with the American view that deterrence must be based on a credible threat that might be realistically implemented. Such a threat could not be based on a swift move to deadly nuclear exchanges.

The compromise of flexible response allowed for tactical nuclear weapons to be kept in Europe as a means of linking the US nuclear arsenal with the defence of Europe. In return the Europeans accepted that there could be no rush into the use of these weapons and that they had to be kept in reserve until conventional action had patently failed. (This was despite the fact that some planners feared that the location of nuclear artillery close to the front could mean that use might be forced upon NATO because of the risk of either preemption or simply being overrun.)

The compromise did not quite resolve the tension between US and European views. For the Europeans the key thing about tactical nuclear weapons was that they were nuclear, American and based on the continent. The 'tactical' side was not so interesting except as a means of entangling the two superpowers in a nuclear exchange against their better judgement. In the 1960s the Americans were prepared to lump all nuclear weapons together and keep them as far as possible to one side in any conflict. In the 1970s, however, the American view changed. If these weapons had to be based in Europe then there ought to be some concepts governing their use. Moreover, the original weapons were now getting old and needing replacement. If they were not replaced then their obsolescence would diminish whatever deterrent effect they offered. If they were to be replaced then their ostensible purpose had to be taken seriously. Could there be 'tactics' for tactical nuclear weapons?

WAR-FIGHTING AND SIGNALLING

During the 1970s this problem was discussed actively in NATO. In some ways the actual development of these discussions was hidden by a change in terminology. 'Tactical' was replaced by 'theatre'. The change reflected embarrassment with the suggestion implied by the term 'tactical' that these weapons could be used as if they were perfectly normal instruments of war. The term 'theatre' recognised that these were weapons that might be employed in a particular 'theatre of war'. It also widened the concept to include longer-range weapons (aircraft and missiles) which tended to get forgotten, fitting awkwardly in between the battlefield 'tactical' weapons and the 'strategic' intercontinental weapons.

The debate within NATO tended to be organised around two distinct approaches to the problem: there were those who believed that theatre nuclear weapons could be used to supplement conventional forces and serve actually to defeat and repel a Soviet invasion, and those who were sceptical of this but felt that use of these weapons might force the aggressor to reconsider by indicating that the alliance was prepared to contemplate nuclear war. These two approaches were characterised as 'war-fighting' and 'signalling' respectively.

The criticisms that the 'signallers' made of the 'war-fighters' can be gleaned from our earlier comments: nuclear weapons cannot be used in a precise and discriminating manner on the battlefield; they would cause immense damage to the surrounding civilian population; any initial advantages accruing from their use would soon be negated by Soviet retaliation and this in turn could lead to further escalation and soon all-out nuclear exchanges.

The counter-critique was that the signallers' proposed actions were barely credible. By exploding a few nuclear weapons all that was being signalled was an unwillingness to accept the logic of a weak strategic position. An extremely limited nuclear use would be of little help to the hard-pressed commanders in the field, who might hope that judicious use of nuclear fire-power might relieve the pressure on their troops, yet, by ending the restraint on nuclear use, would remove whatever inhibitions the USSR might have felt about employing its own nuclear arms. Soviet doctrine does not consider such unmilitary concepts as signalling. The implication of Soviet literature on the use of nuclear weapons in combat is that once employed they will be used en masse against a whole range of military targets. Thus all that would be achieved by signalling would be that the advantage of the first blow would have been squandered.

In both cases the criticism seems persuasive. Neither option is compelling because it is not possible to explain how nuclear use could turn the course of a land battle or the minds of the aggressors without the risk of the conflict quickly generating into the holocaust. The problem is of devising a rational strategy for the employment of nuclear weapons, when any employment is suicidal in its implications. It is hard to believe that a rational nuclear strategy can even be found, in which case nuclear deterrence involves convincing the other side that there are circumstances when rationality could not be assumed. This is not necessarily as difficult as is assumed for there are few circumstances less conducive to rational thought than a massive clash of arms in the centre of Europe. The approach favoured by European governments in the 1960s more or less amounted to this. Nevertheless a strategy based on the possibility of irrational actions in situations rushing out of control is hardly an appealing one for democratic governments to present to their electorates. The flaw with nuclear strategy has not been so much that it is incredible to the USSR, where there might be little difficulty in believing that the west could act in foolish ways, but that it is incredible to those who are supposed to be protected by this strategy.

THE NEUTRON BOMB

For much of the 1970s this lack of public appeal did not seem to matter because the public were not particularly interested in the nuances of nuclear strategy. Moreover, with detente in full swing and arms control agreements being signed, the cold war appeared to be drawing to a sensible close. Nuclear weapons were not to be abolished but at least they were not playing a prominent part in

international conflict, and the superpowers appeared to have resolved to reduce levels of conflict as well as of armaments.

The erosion of detente induced debates in both the United States
and Western Europe over nuclear doctrine. Throughout NATO the
question of 'what do we do if deterrence fails' once again appeared
pertinent. However, the answers to this question were different. In
the United States the debate was led by hawks who argued that the
US lacked a convincing answer, for which they largely blamed the
massive Soviet military build-up that began in 1965. They also
blamed the strategic arms limitation talks (SALT) for obscuring and
even encouraging this dangerous tilt in the strategic balance, and
argued that the position could only be retrieved by a combination of a
massive rearmament programme and the ingenious exploitation of
new nuclear technologies. This debate was largely organised around
SALT, and gained its passion because of the direct responsibility of
the government in Washington for one half of the nuclear arms competition and the fact that it was the occasion for addressing the issue
of general foreign policy towards the USSR.

The debate in Europe took much longer to develop than that in the
US, and gained in intensity because of the impression created by the
American debate. Europeans have little direct control over the state
of nuclear relations in the world yet they stand to lose dramatically by
any breakdown in those relations. There is anxiety in Europe if the
US is too 'soft' with the USSR, with the attendant danger of European interests being sold out, or if it is too 'tough', because then the
risk is of paying the price of an unnecessary confrontation with the
east. As the Asian proverb puts it: the grass gets trampled whether
the elephants fight or make love.

As the 1970s drew to a close, marked by the Soviet invasion of
Afghanistan, the fear in Europe of a superpower confrontation grew.
And this fear seemed to be even more warranted as it came to be
increasingly believed that the US was convinced that it could eventually prevail in any confrontation with the USSR by fighting a limited
nuclear war all over Europe. The evidence for this could be found in
the trend in US strategic doctrine and, more ominous still, in new
weapons to be based on the continent.

The new weapons that prompted this alarm were first the 'neutron
bomb' and second the cruise and Pershing missiles. The neutron
bomb first achieved prominence in 1977 when it was described, quite
inaccurately, as a weapon that kills people but leaves buildings intact.
In fact, it is a weapon that enhances one nuclear effect – prompt

radiation – while reducing others such as blast and fall-out. It is therefore less destructive to buildings than other nuclear weapons that emit equivalent amounts of radiation – but it is destructive enough. This weapon was designed for attacks on tank crews. It was part of a family of 'tailored munitions' which were supposed to be able to offer the discrimination that earlier generations of battlefields nuclear weapons lacked – they would hit the target with only limited collateral damage to surrounding areas and people.

Enhanced radiation weapons, as they were known in NATO argot, had been moving through the alliance planning processes without attracting much attention as replacements for obsolete nuclear artillery shells and warheads for short-range missiles. They had not been subjected to much scrutiny. Yet a powerful case could have been deployed against them. They would solve none of the basic problems of battlefield nuclear weapons: they were not more like conventional weapons, since they concentrated on the most nuclear of nuclear effects – intense and lethal radiation; they would be subject to the special treatment of this category of weapons and so use would probably not be authorised at the most appropriate time and the need to use large numbers to cope with dispersed enemy tank formations would still result in large-scale collateral damage; the probability of Soviet retaliation would remain. Even if these weapons might succeed in blurring the boundaries between conventional and nuclear weapons, there were the long-standing arguments as to whether the undermining of a clear firebreak (or nuclear threshold) was desirable.

Points such as these were made by some of the critics of the 'neutron bomb', but the main furore was over the erroneous notion that this was a bomb designed to protect property (a capitalist bomb no less!) with the implication that it was to be used to generate eerie death rays in major cities that would wipe out the population but leave the buildings standing as a silent prize for invading forces. Or else a vague disgust was communicated that something even more horrible than ordinary nuclear weapons had been invented, that the Americans were responsible and that the Europeans were expected to be the passive hosts to this new form of evil.

The neutron bomb was the object of widespread repugnance and this encouraged the revival of the anti-nuclear protest movements in Europe. NATO tried to prepare the ground for its introduction but without great conviction. In April 1978 President Carter decided that he did not wish to be associated with the thing and decided against deployment. Although preparations for production went ahead, and in 1981 the Reagan administration decided on full-scale production, the reputation of the weapon was now so low that European governments, with anti-nuclear campaigns now even more active, did not dare to agree to deployment on the continent.

CRUISE MISSILES

The campaign against the neutron bomb was the prelude to a much more substantial campaign against NATO's long-range theatre nuclear force (LRTNF) modernisation programme, based on 464 Tomahawk cruise missiles and 108 Pershing ballistic missiles, agreed in December 1979. The curious feature of this campaign is that many arguments that might have been deployed effectively against the neutron bomb, but were neglected, were now deployed against these long-range missiles, where they were largely invalid. Thus it has been argued that once implemented this new programme would enable the United States to fight a 'limited nuclear war', in which Europe but not North America would suffer – the weapons which kill Europe but leave the superpowers intact!

The whole point about the cruise and Pershing missiles was that they were designed to increase the nuclear risk to the United States of a land war in Europe. The reasoning may be as arcane as much else in NATO doctrine, but it is important to understand the motives of the policy-makers responsible. In the 1977–8 period, when the issue was first gaining political attention, the question was seen to be one of reinforcing the link between the US nuclear arsenal and the defence of Europe, long deemed essential to the strategy of flexible response. The idea was to accentuate the possibilities for escalation, confirming that any war would in all probability come to involve both superpowers in nuclear exchanges. Long-range American weapons capable of attacking Soviet targets are hardly instruments of limited war. This is why the initial political impulse for the programme came from Europe and not from the US. As we have seen, it comes well within the curious strategic tradition of flexible response.

The campaigns against the LRTNF programme that have developed in Europe only grudgingly acknowledge European responsibility for the project or the practical implausibility of cruise and Pershing missiles as instruments of limited war. In a way NATO has been caught in an inverted version of its own arguments on the psychology of deterrence. If what matters is what the USSR thinks about NATO capabilities and intentions more than what we think is actually the case, then the same can be true of the US. *We may know* that limited nuclear war is an erroneous concept and that, even if it were not, cruise missiles would be an inappropriate instrument for such a war, but is this understood in Washington? The risk is that the US could be lulled by its own foolish theories of nuclear strategy into the belief that a nuclear war could be won without great damage to itself.

It is beyond the scope of this chapter to discuss how the US managed to acquire such a reputation for recklessness and miscalculation, but any observer of the recent European debates cannot but be aware of this reputation. The post-Afghanistan belligerence in US foreign policy and the rhetoric of the Reagan administration have not conveyed a sense of moderation. However the actual behaviour in foreign policy has been much more cautious than the rhetoric and there is no evidence to support the image of a United States anxious for war. Moreover the statements by members of the administration, including the President himself, about the possibly limited character of a European nuclear war are no more than NATO commonplaces that have only been noticed because of the sensitivity of the issues. It has always been possible that nuclear exchanges might stop after a few explosions. Presumably this, while still horrific, would be preferable to unlimited nuclear war. It would be reasonable to expect NATO leaders to attempt to fight any war with as much restraint as possible. The issue is whether sufficient confidence might be generated that a war could definitely be limited to create a temptation to try to find out if this is so. Nobody knows how a nuclear war will be fought, so one man's speculation is as good or bad as another. The worry is the man who believes he knows and is prepared to act on this knowledge.

FIRST STRIKES

Here certain trends in US strategic writing have given grounds for concern. During the 1970s US strategists have doggedly attempted to square the circle of NATO doctrine. As we have already made clear the dilemma of NATO doctrine is how to make it all credible to the potential aggressor that a US President would authorise use of nuclear weapons in circumstances where NATO is being defeated in conventional war. This dilemma intensifies the more likely it is that

NATO would suffer such a defeat and the more that the Europeans insist that NATO must not even pretend that a war cannot be contained at a conventional level. Nuclear strategy is only intellectually manageable when the object is no more than to deter a nuclear strike against one's own territory by means of the threat of retaliation. When one tries to do more than that one soon comes to the question of what could possibly be the rationality of responding to a severe but one-sided loss by making it virtually inevitable that the loss would be catastrophic even if shared.

The obvious way out is to disarm the enemy by a surprise attack – the so-called 'first strike'. It must be clear that, precisely defined, a successful first-strike must remove virtually all of the enemy's effective means of retaliation. It does not mean first use of nuclear weapons nor does it refer to a number of super-accurate weapons capable of knocking out a portion of the enemy's retaliatory forces. A collection of accurate weapons is a necessary but barely sufficient condition for a first strike. The ability to destroy a protected target is of slight relevance if the missile is so slow that it is likely to be detected and interrupted before reaching its target, as is the cruise missile. So there is no such thing as a 'first strike weapon': a 'first strike' must refer to a total capability. Such a capability, if it ever did exist, certainly does not exist for either side under current conditions. Nor is it likely to develop in the foreseeable future. This is because of the sheer number and variety of offensive systems and, most importantly, the mobility of key systems such as submarines. Despite what is commonly believed about the US or the USSR planning for highly destabilising first strike capabilities, there is no indication that either considers such an option to be within reach. The problem comes back to that of what is believed to be true, or even what is believed about what the other side believes to be true, often being more important than the reality. If it is suspected that the other side considers itself in sight of some decisive war-winning nuclear capability then compensating measures become necessary to fortify deterrence. The 'you can never be too sure' type of argument always seems compelling when the stakes are so high. Chapters 1 and 2 deal with the need to structure forces to discourage all alarms over first strike plans. This task becomes easier if it is combined with a rigorous effort to keep alarms of this sort in perspective.

There has undoubtedly been a lot of concern recently about first strikes, largely a result of using the term extremely loosely or of assuming that there would be some point in a partial first strike that left a large chunk of the enemy's means of retaliation intact.

Exchanges in which land-based missiles would try to catch each other on the ground have been postulated but nobody has yet explained convincingly the purpose of such exchanges. It has been more a case of watching a capability develop, because of the technological push of multiple warheads and improved guidance, and then reading into it some dark strategic intent. This is what happened in the United States during the 1970s as there was a rapid proliferation of warheads on the Soviet side. US ICBMs were seen to be rendered increasingly vulnerable. Instead of taking comfort in the good survival prospects of their many other delivery systems, such as submarines, American strategists began to get themselves into an awful pickle and explored schemes of stupendous complexity, ingenuity, cost and, eventually, futility, to save ICBMs from threat. The classic example of this was the MX missile for which a new basing mode had to be designed each summer. None provided the required survivability.

In a similar manner some had read some mischievous first strike purposes into the proposal to base cruise and Pershing missiles in Europe. We have already noted that the slow cruise missiles which take hours to reach their targets would be unsuitable for this task. However, more concern has been expressed about the Pershing which could reach certain Soviet missile sites and associated command centres in a few minutes. It has been suggested that even if there is a limit to what might be achieved by 108 Pershings against 1400 Soviet missiles, most of which are out of range, the prospect of this rapid attack will force the USSR towards a 'launch-on-warning' capability. The fact that Soviet leaders seem more worried by Pershing than cruise adds weight to this argument.

Launch-on-warning is a frightening prospect for it suggests that rather than riding out an attack to ensure that it does actually involve nuclear weapons and is not a false alarm, the warning systems will be sufficiently trusted to permit the launch of a retaliatory strike before the relevant systems have been caught on the ground. Neither side has ever explicitly disowned this doctrine: value has been seen in letting the other side suspect that any attack will just destroy holes in the ground that have already been emptied of their contents. The Americans have looked upon this sort of approach with disfavour, believing it puts far too much reliance on warning systems. By contrast, since the mid-1960s, there have been a number of Soviet statements indicating adoption of launch-on-warning. In this case it may be that the problem posed by Pershing for the USSR is not that it pushes them towards this dangerous doctrine, but that it makes it more difficult for them to implement. Twenty minutes (the journey for an ICBM from the US to the USSR) is long enough to assess an incoming attack and to decide to respond, but five minutes (the journey for Pershing) is not.

Which all goes to show that in the confused world of nuclear planning nothing is ever quite what it seems. Carefully composed operations implied by such terms as 'first strike' are never likely to be possible to implement in such a way that would impress a political leader to go ahead. The term is outdated – it refers to what might have been an option if technology had taken a different course twenty years ago. The problem is not 'first strike' but another approach with which it is often confused – 'first use'.

The problem that the strategists have been facing stem from the fact that there is no way of removing the retaliatory threat. Because they are trying to inject credibility into the threat to use nuclear weapons first, they have sought methods of fighting a nuclear war without invoking great retaliation. Thus the whole debate about signalling and limited war-fighting, the strange scenarios of demonstration shots, of selective strikes against KGB headquarters or economic assets or command and control networks, or of competitive counterforce attacks. All these strategies have been attempts to insert some muscle and credibility into NATO's new doctrine. The attempt may have been futile, and ought now to be acknowledged to have failed, but the motive was nothing more sinister than a desire to meet requirements set by NATO doctrine. It is extremely difficult to find an official of NATO or of a member country who advocates limited nuclear strikes or a decisive war-winning strategy. All that is argued is that when under pressure and contemplating 'going nuclear' it is better that NATO has available some limited options, however implausible, other than resort to all-out counter-city exchanges.

Thus neither the proposed deployments of cruise and Pershing missiles nor the ferment in strategic thinking represent major new departures in western plans. Nevertheless, because of the publicity generated, they have helped draw attention to the inadequacies in NATO doctrine. Once one begins to explain a strategy based on the threat of first use then alarm bells start to ring. The awkwardness of the NATO establishment in explaining its position properly betrays the awkwardness of the position it has to defend.

But like the neutron bomb, the opportunity to pinpoint a long-standing flaw in NATO strategy (for which the Europeans have been largely responsible) was obscured by the desire of the campaigners to use the missile issue to make a series of charges concerning the supposed nuclear malevolence and recklessness of the United States.

Moreover, the fervent criticisms of NATO 'limited war' doctrine, pointing to the inevitability of escalation to devastation or the horrors of even limited nuclear employment, were to a large extent pushing at an open door. The problem with NATO doctrine is not that it is unaware of the probability of escalation but that the only way it can use this probability to reinforce deterrence is to attempt to create circumstances in which NATO might, despite the dictates of common sense, embark upon nuclear exchanges as an alternative to conventional defeat. Although the USSR may be sufficiently convinced of western irrationality not to take chances, this doctrine of first nuclear use does not commend itself as being credible and is certainly not comforting.

A NEW APPROACH

Where does this leave us? I have argued that the presentation of the proposed cruise missile programme as a US imposition on supine European members of NATO in order to prepare for limited nuclear war (or first strikes) is nonsense. The origins of the programme are to be found in the European insistence since the 1950s that NATO must depend above all on nuclear deterrence, and that the unavoidable doubts concerning the US nuclear guarantee can only be eased by entangling US nuclear forces as closely and visibly as possible with the territorial defence of Western Europe. It is this set of European attitudes that provides the source of the problem of NATO's over-dependence on nuclear weapons.

Can this situation be remedied? The key no longer lies in new variations on the discredited themes of nuclear strategy. No amount of amateur psychology or intellectual obscurantism can hide the hopelessness of relying for security on a threat of nuclear first use. The main issue is whether there are new forms of conventional strategy that can allow us to have more confidence that a Soviet invasion could be repelled without resort to nuclear weapons, a prospect which, if impressed on the USSR, ought to ensure deterrence.

We have noted in our discussion up to now two basic arguments against a shift to a conventional strategy: (1) it is too expensive to do it properly; (2) by itself, conventional war is not an awesome enough prospect to sustain deterrence. To answer (1) it is necessary to consider just what is involved in doing it properly. There is now within NATO general agreement that it is important to improve conventional forces, and that this involves looking at reserves, stocks, force structure, new technologies and so on. The issue has become one of degree – can one improve sufficiently to remove completely dependence on the threat of first nuclear use or does it just allow the alliance to consider no *early* first nuclear use.

There is at the moment a lot of research under way within the NATO countries on the various means by which NATO might improve its conventional forces at limited, or even no extra cost. Years of preoccupation with nuclear strategy, often of a curiously and distastefully eccentric nature, have led to a neglect of conventional strategy. While nuclear strategy has often been marked by novelty for its own sake, the designs and deployment of conventional forces still follow traditional concepts. The renewed attention to this area ought to illuminate possibilities for reform.

The Warsaw Pact, with its own internal tensions, may not be as unmanageable a threat as is often assumed. It is probably that Warsaw Pact military capabilities have been exaggerated by concentrating on quantities of troops and equipment without due regard for their quality. The best Soviet divisions, which would be to the fore of any invasion, may be as good as any in the world but there are likely to be important deficiencies in those coming up behind. The Eastern European satellites could well be reluctant and unreliable allies (though not necessarily so if, for example, West Germany can be convincingly portrayed as the villain of the piece). For its own part, the USSR will probably be more impressed with the quality of the NATO forces facing it than are the NATO countries themselves, and when it comes to deterrence it is the Soviet perceptions that matter.

Furthermore, any major aggression in contemporary conditions would be, more than ever, a leap into the dark. It would be a war fought with armies and weapons that are largely untested in political and military circumstances that would generate sufficient uncertainties to confuse even the most clear-headed tactician. We know little of how armies can cope with battles that can be conducted night and day, whatever the weather, without opportunity for respite under cover and with high rates of attrition. The logistics and command systems are crucial to the conduct of war, despite being neglected in pre-war assessments. On how robust they prove to be during actual combat, and how great the capacity for improvisation by the fighting forces when they fail, much will depend.

Yet even while both those possibilities may keep the military problem down to size, the question of cost will still loom extremely large. Those politicians who are particularly anxious to reduce dependence on nuclear weapons often insist that they would be prepared to argue for increased expenditure on conventional forces. Savings could be made by removing battlefield nuclear weapons, for example in easing the requirements for their security and command and control, or by releasing dual-capable artillery and aircraft for a dedicated conventional role. However, the fact is that nuclear fire-power comes cheaper than conventional fire-power and those who will the end of a credible conventional strategy must be prepared to will the means. It is not entirely improper for military cynics to ask whether when it came to the crunch there would be general approbation for increased reliance on conventional forces and an equally general reluctance to vote the necessary funds.

The second objection – making Europe safe for conventional war – is both more substantial and less difficult. One of the curious consequences of the preoccupation with nuclear weapons is that all other types of weapons appear moderate by comparison. Moreover talking of 'conventional war' implies a set of engagements that would be governed according to recognised and understood 'conventions' so that we are describing traditional war-fighting. If deterrence is about implanting a sense of the horror and uncertainty of war in the minds of those who might be tempted to launch one, then maybe conventional warfare appears too tolerable and manageable. Such an impression should not be difficult to dispel. Conventional warfare in the centre of Europe is an extremely nasty and unpredictable prospect and this in itself constitutes an important deterrent. To propose a conventional strategy is to propose a lesser evil – significantly lesser but still significantly evil.

What would this mean for nuclear forces? The objective of the sort of strategic shift described here would be to remove from NATO the intellectual and moral burden of relying for its defence on the need to stress a threat of first use of nuclear weapons. The role of the NATO nuclear arsenal is then left to one of deterring the use of the other's nuclear arsenal. This means that survivable forces are necessary to ensure that there is no risk of being caught in a first strike. The need for nuclear weapons capable of performing a variety of subtle military tasks. However, just as it would be unwise to pretend that a nuclear war could be fought in a particularly discriminating manner, it would also be unwise to pretend that in the middle of a fierce, bitter and confused land war in Europe one can guarantee by means of prior declaration that nuclear weapons definitely will not be used. Furthermore, the very possibility that nuclear weapons might be used imposes important constraints on conventional offensive plans (i.e. enforcing dispersion).

In the first instance the best move that NATO could make would be to turn over artillery to conventional purposes and remove nuclear artillery shells from their European storage sites back to the United States. Such a move would remove those weapons that represent NATO doctrine at its most confusing and alarming and which provide the greatest risk of premature nuclear employment. It is also the case that many of the military tasks assigned to battlefield nuclear weapons can now be accomplished by conventional weapons.

If one removes the battlefield weapons (which incidentally, I believe, should be undertaken as part of a NATO programme and not as a measure of arms control) this provides an argument for longer-range theatre nuclear forces. So long as the USSR has nuclear weapons dedicated to European targets it will be necessary to have weapons available to respond in kind. If all nuclear weapons were withdrawn from Western European soil a Soviet leader might just be tempted by the thought that a nuclear attack on NATO would be unlikely to lead to the launching of American intercontinental missiles. However intellectually unconvincing, US deployments of nuclear weapons in Europe do provide a tangible symbol of the depth of the US commitment to the defence of the continent.

ARMS CONTROL

The strategic shift advocated here does not depend on any achievements in arms control. NATO must have a doctrine with which its people can feel comfortable and forces that are seen to be neither excessive nor provocative. Indeed, if NATO had a clearer doctrine then that would facilitate arms control because it would offer more guidance on where systems could sensibly be cut and where particular capabilities might have to be maintained.

At the moment arms control proposals lack the benefit of a clear theory of security. There is a dangerous tendency for politicians to advocate it as an attempt to show good faith in their willingness to seek out diplomatic solutions to security problems. In doing so it is hoped to placate the anti-nuclear movements. Unfortunately experience has shown that while negotiations with clear and realisable objectives can produce results, where the objectives are less certain the result is negotiations of great length and tedium which produce little but cynicism. There is a risk of elevating military trivia and technicalities into sensitive issues that aggravates rather than overcomes mistrust.

The preceding analysis does set some guidelines for arms control. The most serious and difficult requirement is for action at the conventional level. If the two sides are not going to rely excessively on nuclear arms, then they must be encouraged to find security in conventional forces. As these forces are extremely expensive, anything that can encourage reductions in force levels is to be welcomed. There have been negotiations underway in Vienna for ten years to achieve such reductions, but they have got caught up in a row over data that may prove to be their undoing. Both NATO and the Warsaw Pact agree that there can be reductions to an agreed level of troop numbers. Both believe in parity. Unfortunately Warsaw Pact figures show an existing parity which implies a need for equal reductions, while NATO figures show Warsaw Pact superiority which leads to a demand for unequal reductions. As the discrepancy is large – some 150 000 troops – this problem is going to be extremely difficult to resolve. There are other areas where conventional arms control can be discussed – such as the follow-on conferences of the 1975 Helsinki Conferences on Security and Cooperation in Europe. But these concentrate on confidence-building measures (CBMs) which are largely concerned with prior notification or observation of any troop movements, and particularly full-scale manoeuvres, lest they suddenly turn into something nasty. These measures can be useful in making it difficult to mount surprise attacks, but they do not offer the prospect of actual disarmament.

On the nuclear side there is a lot of activity but a lack of direction. There are now negotiations underway at Geneva on both strategic (which is normally taken to mean intercontinental) and intermediate nuclear forces. The strategic talks are the latest stage in a long-running saga, and are dealt with fully in the chapter by Edwina Moreton. The intermediate nuclear forces (INF) talks are quite new. They represent an attempt to meet NATO's objective, as set out in the December 1979 decision which announced plans to introduce cruise and Pershing missiles, to explore the possibilities of arms control in this area. This was always an uncertain objective. On the one hand it inevitably encouraged the making of strict comparisons with the Soviet missile, the SS-20, both in numbers and capabilities. On the other hand, NATO's deployment was ostensibly meeting a unique NATO requirement. The Warsaw Pact's geography and political structure ensure that the coupling of Soviet security to that of its allies is not an issue. For NATO this linkage is a perennial problem, and the cruise and Pershing missiles were supposed to help by coupling a defence of Europe on land with US nuclear forces. Even if there were no Soviet medium-range missiles there would still be an argument for NATO missiles.

However the actual situation at the start of the 1980s was the reverse: there were large numbers of Soviet missiles and aircraft targeted on Western Europe and only a limited number of aircraft based on European soil able to attack targets in the Soviet Union. NATO's bargaining position was not impressive. All it had to offer was the possibility of scaling down or cancelling the 572 new missiles that were to be introduced during the 1980s, and Moscow might reasonably suspect that the pressures of the anti-nuclear movement would achieve that objective for them. In return for not going ahead with its paper plans, NATO would require reductions and limits on existing Soviet missiles (around 250 MIRVed SS-20s each with three warheads, and some 300 older SS-4s and SS-5s), including those located east of the Urals – based outside of the European area yet able to hit targets in Europe.

It would be unrealistic to pretend that in any circumstances this combination of forces lends itself to agreement. Either NATO has to live with an imbalance in the Soviet Union's favour, or the USSR has to reduce its force substantially and unilaterally. The Reagan administration made the best of a bad job by proposing a 'zero option' by which NATO would cancel the cruise and Pershing missile programmes in return for the removal of all SS-4, SS-5 and SS-20 missiles. It was never likely to be accepted and, if it had been, it would contradict the original rationale for the programme. But it had the advantage of disorienting the peace movement by appropriating its slogan – 'no cruise; no SS-20'. Those whose whole approach to disarmament has been theatrical and determined not to be constrained by the problems of negotiations found themselves worrying that the American position was insufficiently realistic.

If anything does emerge from the INF talks it is unlikely to resemble the zero option. It would be unwise to pretend that much is likely to emerge from these talks as presently constituted. At the moment the US wants to confine the talks to missiles but expand the geographical scope to cover the Asian part of the USSR as well as the European part. Because of the triple warhead on the SS-20 the US wants to count warheads rather than just launchers. The USSR, as might be expected, wants to count launchers in Europe. It, however, wishes to include British and French systems as well as American, and aircraft as well as missiles. (The aircraft question does not actually work in the Soviet favour, except that the USSR insists on counting the opposing forces in a curious way.)

This does not mean that a deal cannot be struck. The USSR might be willing to make substantial concessions to achieve a cancellation of the Pershing programme. The two sides might come to a political understanding at a summit meeting in which they would each abandon 'sticking points' in order to achieve agreement. Another possibility would be to integrate the INF talks with the strategic arms talks. There is much to be said for this option. It is already proving extremely difficult to keep the two negotiations distinct – cruise missiles or the Backfire bomber, for example, might come under either heading. There is a logical link between the two: a Pershing II or an SS-20 are as 'strategic' as a Minuteman or SS-19 ICBM despite the shorter range. For the European members of NATO this sort of link would achieve in negotiating terms what they have always tried to achieve in doctrine – a lack of distinction between US nuclear forces intended to deter attack on North America and those to deter attack in Western Europe. Joining the two sets of negotiations might just provide a greater degree of flexibility and allow for trades that would not be possible if the two were kept separate.

All that being said, there are no real grounds for optimism. There is a great risk that the hopes now invested in the INF talks will not be realised. Or at least if they are realised at all it will only be after a substantial delay and with an outcome that may not be very impressive in terms of alteration to established capabilities and plans. This would have three unfortunate consequences. First, such a failure would discredit arms control and put its supporters on the defensive, even though INF is not a good test for a concept which works best when set limited and modest tasks. Second, it will discourage new initiatives. The need for some sort of move on battlefield nuclear weapons has been mentioned. In many ways these shorter-range weapons are even more unpromising than the long-range ones as subjects for negotiation: they come in all shapes and sizes, are difficult to verify and are not held symmetrically by the two sides. Yet there are some interesting ideas around for their control – such as the one proposed by the Independent Commission on Security and Disarmament issues chaired by Olaf Palme of Sweden. This would have 150 km zone along the east–west divide in which these weapons would be prohibited. This limited step would at least ensure a delay in consideration of the use of these weapons.

The third consequence is that any recriminations following the failure of arms control and possibly the failure of the modernisation programme could put further strain on the Atlantic alliance. The programme began with the idea that this would be a way of reaffirming the US commitment to European security. It would be tragic if a political failure in the implementation of the programme helped to cast doubt on the American willingness to make that commitment or the European willingness to accept it. As many in the anti-nuclear movement would undoubtedly consider it an enormous bonus should their efforts bring about a collapse of the alliance, we need now to examine the political foundations of the current argument.

ALLIANCES

To those who accept the framework set by NATO, the sort of approach advocated in this chapter might seem quite sensible, but to others it will be hardly satisfactory. Somehow it fails to address the deeper fears and anxieties that animate much of the anti-nuclear protest and the general public concern. It is all well and good to make NATO strategy more credible in military terms and less reckless when it comes to nuclear weapons, but none of this actually removes the nuclear menace or heals the east–west divide that might one day turn this menace into a horrifying reality.

We have been discussing a strategic shift away from short-range to long-range nuclear weapons and the strengthening of conventional deterrence. This is of relevance only if one defines the problem to start with in terms of military relations. The same is really true of the arguments about 'first strike weapons'. The issue raised is whether a particular relationship of military forces is stabilising or not. Is there a danger that a political crisis will get driven by military factors so that, for example, a rush to mobilise or a fear of preemptive strike undermines and bypasses diplomacy and turns something that might have been settled peacefully into war? Once war has begun might the proximity of nuclear weapons to the border and their integration into ground forces precipitate nuclear use before the situation warranted even considering such a step? The proposals associated with arms control seek to address these sort of questions.

The case for the prosecution outlined at the start of this chapter argued that the problem runs much deeper: the nuclear issue is bound up with the question of the division of Europe into overarmed alliances, each dominated by a superpower. Stabilising military relationships is to attempt to fix them in time, accepting the political conflict that created them as being permanent. It seeks to keep matters steady at weapons of certain types and numbers lest they be replaced by something worse. The question is whether this uneasy division of Europe into two overarmed alliances can be sustained indefinitely without a head-on collision. Much of the current concern has been over supposedly mischievous developments in weaponry and strategy, so it has been a minimum objective of the protestors to oppose these developments. I have argued that the situation in this sense is not as dire as many suspect and that remedies are at hand which could visibly reduce NATO's dependence on nuclear threat. It is probably the case that the diversity of nuclear systems and the uncertainties surrounding any military operation that might trigger their use have created a situation of utter military paralysis and therefore of considerable stability. Neither side can contemplate an attack on the other and really expect to get away with it. And this will remain so within a wide range of alternative force structures and military balances. Adjustments to nuclear force levels, whether upwards or downwards, in practical military terms, within obvious limits, are pretty inconsequential. But let us suppose that those who fear that NATO's nuclear plans threaten something terribly dangerous get their way: cruise missiles are abandoned and NATO leaders agree in all solemnity to reject all thoughts of limited nuclear war and all threats of nuclear first strikes. Should we then feel safe?

To return to the question with which this chapter started, is there any reason why we should feel less safe now than twenty years ago? It is true that the stockpiles have grown and the individual weapons have become more sophisticated, but it is the degree of political conflict that really determines the general sense of anxiety. In the late 1950s and early 1960s with the post-war boundaries of Europe still unsettled and the status of Berlin constantly in dispute there was more reason for worry. And war then would not have been notably less awful than it would now. The series of agreements that marked the start of detente in the late 1960s and early 1970s involved more than attempts at arms control: they actually sorted out all these disputes over borders and the position of Berlin. This was largely achieved by recognising the post-war stalemate. Attempts to alter the status quo were not going to be worth the attendant risks. West Germany and East Germany acknowledged the separate existence of each other.

Even though the spirit of detente has now faded, there are lasting achievements which have made Europe far safer than it was. The significance of the Helsinki agreements of 1975 was in removing from Europe nagging fears that someone would try to redraw the boundaries. The achievement was negative but substantial. It was not followed by positive achievements – such as liberalisation of the communist countries, or a breaking down of other east–west political divisions. Where progress was made, in economic relations, this soon faltered on the differences between the two systems, most especially the lack of competitiveness of the East. As Eastern European countries imported western technology they did not so much improve the productivity of their industry as saddle themselves with enormous debt. Even more seriously, the USSR seemed to view detente as a very limited exercise, and not applying to the Third World.

Much of the recent nervousness in Europe stems from the awareness that the high hopes that accompanied detente in the 1970s have not been realised, and that the collapse of its spirit has been marked by fierce rhetoric and denunciations. The fear is that renewed US–USSR antagonism will lead to an unravelling of the understandings reached in Europe and a dangerous breakdown of relations. Yet the basic agreements remain intact. It is not true to say that we are 'returning to the cold war', because far more was in dispute between east and west up to the mid-1960s than is the case now. What appears to have happened is that the system of alliances which is on the surface all about preparation for conflict has turned into a means of managing conflict. Both sides know where their area begins and where it ends. Neither attempts to trespass. In a curious way the division of Europe has disciplined its political life.

This undoubtedly has a cost. In return for the USSR desisting from attempts to extend its hegemony over us, we find ourselves frustrated in our desire to help fellow-Europeans unfortunate enough to be in the Soviet sphere of influence. When the Poles struggle for freedom they do so alone. Indeed we find ourselves torn by the logic of our instincts which demands a break-up of the Soviet Empire in Eastern Europe and the logic of security which warns that the process of breaking up could set in motion a frightful chain of events that could end in war and disaster. In practice we cannot adopt a stance of unremitting conservatism, arguing against any change in political relations lest it upset the European balance. Change is a constant. So the challenge for European security is to adapt to change, recognising the strains within both alliances.

So long as the system of alliances backed up by a military paralysis and the fear of nuclear war remains viable, it should not be rejected lightly. Furthermore, it should be acknowledged that many of the specific measures embraced with enthusiasm by arms controllers and disarmers alike offer no more than an attempt to shore up the status quo by keeping military relations in check. The constant preoccupation with 'stability' is a giveaway. Worries about preemptive strikes and arms races reflect a fundamentally conservative objective: to allow the existing political relationship to continue without either side feeling able to transform it by military means. But the political and military potential for an east–west nuclear war remains.

NUCLEAR-FREE ZONES

This brings us to a dilemma for the anti-nuclear movement. Does it want to calm the passions and cool the rhetoric and return the great powers to detente and sensible measures of arms control, or does it have something more radical in mind? The detail of its proposals suggests the former, but the language of its campaign conveys the latter. This conservatism cannot suffice. Mass demonstrations are not called to facilitate marginal adjustments in power politics. Passionate pleas and indignant demands are not raised to achieve the trimming or the reorganisation of the nuclear arsenals. The cause is much grander. For the 'peace' movement, the European security system must be transformed. The nuclear weapons must be removed altogether and the fracture down the middle of the continent must be healed. The aspiration is captured by the slogan of a 'nuclear-free zone from Poland to Portugal'.

The concept of a nuclear-free zone has to be treated as both a technical and a political proposition. The technical objections are straightforward and many would consider them decisive: the range and mobility of modern weapons mocks any attempt to limit their geographical impact. Europe can be attacked from west of the Rockies or east of the Urals. The only nuclear-free zones that would really matter would be the US and the USSR. European safety will always be relative while they are nuclear-loaded. It is simply not the case that only nuclear facilities provide the targets for another's nuclear weapons. It is a joke in doubtful taste for local councils to declare themselves nuclear-free and then to mark this liberation by abandoning civil defence preparations. This may say something about the power of positive thinking but in the event of war their people would be in for a rude shock.

The political objections are more significant. A zone from 'Poland to Portugal' bears no relation to any existing political reality. It assumes a natural break in Europe at the Polish–Soviet border and ignores the very real break that runs through the middle of Europe. For those seduced by this slogan it is vital to realise that the withdrawal of nuclear weapons from the continent would not suddenly lift up all the barriers that divide nations. Even if it helped to break up the alliance systems, old divisions, fears, suspicions and aspirations would be revived. Europe would not become one big happy family but would in all probability start to reflect the unease of the non-German states as to the strength and position of a reunited Germany.

However, the alliances now have social, political and economic roots that will remain even when the weapons are gone. The problem we have with the east is not the result of some unfortunate misunderstanding. It reflects a real difference in ideology that matters a great deal if we value at all our way of life and democratic freedoms. By disarming ourselves and dismantling our alliances we would not encourage the USSR to follow suit. It would just be able to hold on to its empire at a slightly lower level of forces. But hold on to its empire it must, for the Eastern European states are not only essential to it as a buffer against the west (and in all conceivable circumstances it would want a buffer against Germany) but are essential to its own internal cohesion and the strength and legitimacy of the communist system. The Kremlin has limited room for manoeuvre when it comes to the toleration of change in Eastern Europe. Unfortunately this room does not appear to be dependent on the policies of the west. Indeed when east–west contact was flourishing in the early 1970s, the KGB felt obliged to be even more politically repressive lest the disease of western liberalism be allowed to spread.

To pretend that there can be a protest movement in the east to parallel that in the west is self-delusion. If it is believed that the future course of events will be shaped by the pattern of protest, then it had better be recognised that the result will be extremely one-sided. The suppression of 'Solidarity' in Poland and of the small but independent peace movements in East Germany and the USSR illustrate this sad truth.

We cannot know how the Warsaw Pact will develop over the coming decade. It certainly suffers from great internal strains which require it to be watched with care and treated with caution. What is clear is that the USSR is determined to maintain its grip on its reluctant allies and will only loosen its grip if forced to do so: this will involve political repercussions fraught with danger for us all. Western Europe has no immediate option of a free and easy relation with its eastern neighbours. To pretend that any of the measures advocated by the anti-nuclear movement could bring that about is a cruel deception. The basic political fact of Europe for the rest of this century will be the power of the USSR. The American involvement in Europe is by invitation. The Soviet involvement is by geography. The question for Western Europeans is whether they wish to withdraw their invitation to the US and deal with the USSR on its own terms, or continue to benefit from the nuclear protection offered by the US. They cannot ask the USSR to withdraw. The USSR is a fixture, and so, it would seem, are the nuclear weapons with which it arms itself. To attempt to deal with the USSR by neglecting to mention it in a slogan is tantamount to fraud.

The underlying stability of the current security system should not be underestimated. It cannot be expected to endure forever and the challenge for the future will undoubtedly be to adapt it to the changes in the wider international environment and in the domestic politics of the states which make it up. Yet we accelerate its decomposition at our peril. To remove all the counters to Soviet power before the USSR and its satellites have had a chance to undergo the sort of changes that will make them more congenial neighbours is to invite trouble. If we reject US protection by expelling US nuclear bases then we have to find a way to deal with Soviet nuclear power. One option would be to provide our own nuclear protection, with perhaps Germany becoming the next major nuclear power. Another option would be slowly to accede to Soviet demands out of fear of upsetting this superpower on our doorstep. As concession followed concession we would have time to ponder that to be really nuclear-free is not simply to rid ourselves of the artefacts of the nuclear age, but to be sure that everybody else has done the same.

4 Britain and the Bomb

JOHN BAYLIS

SHOULD BRITAIN POSSESS A STRATEGIC NUCLEAR DETERRENT?

The fact that every government in Britain since World War II has answered yes to this question obviously does not foreclose debate on such a vital issue of the nation's security. Indeed it is right and proper that the reasons behind the expenditure of billions of pounds on weapons capable of killing millions of people should be constantly scrutinised, questioned and subjected to the most rigorous analysis. This is especially so at a time when there is widespread concern in Britain, as in other countries of Western Europe and North America, about the possession of nuclear weapons and current western strategy. The position of Britain is, of course, not unique. Britain was, however, the first country to decide to acquire nuclear weapons, and, if supporters of the new, revitalised Campaign for Nuclear Disarmament (CND) have their way, it would be the first to renounce unilaterally such weapons. As such, Britain provides an interesting case study for this final chapter. We do not claim that arguments which follow are wholly exhaustive but they do at least give the reader some insights into the debate that is currently taking place.

In order to come to a balanced judgement on this crucial question whether to retain a British nuclear deterrent, four supplementary questions must be asked:

1. Is there a threat to Britain?
2. How convincing are the arguments supporting a British nuclear force?
3. Is the moral argument decisive?
4. Can Britain afford nuclear weapons?

This will be followed by a brief discussion of the resurgence of the CND movement and alternative defence policies which might be adopted.

IS THERE A THREAT TO BRITAIN?

At the root of any judgement about whether Britain should possess an independent nuclear deterrent is the question of whether there is a threat to Britain which requires the maintenance of such a force. The threat most usually debated is obviously that from the Soviet Union. Those opposing a British nuclear deterrent, while not necessarily approving of the Soviet regime, usually argue that the Soviet threat has been greatly exaggerated. They point to the relatively cautious use of force by the Soviet leaders outside their borders since 1917; the main exceptions being in areas regarded as largely within their own sphere of influence. They also tend to interpret the build-up of Soviet military power as resulting from an attempt to catch up with the United States, in the course of which the superpowers have become locked in a senseless arms race. According to this view, although the Soviet Union has an unpleasant domestic regime it is largely defensively orientated and anyway it has enough problems on its plate at home and in its dependencies to prevent it from threatening Western Europe. Such a view tends to suggest that ideology plays a relatively small part in Soviet calculations and that certainly the Soviet Union is not bent on world domination. The implication of this judgement is that Soviet behaviour is the result of national insecurity and traditional overinsurance which can best be dealt with by a less hawkish response from the west and by unilateral actions to demonstrate western goodwill. It must be said that this is not the only interpretation of the Soviet Union held by those seeking to renounce British nuclear weapons but it is nevertheless the most common one.

Any attempt to interpret Soviet motivation and to assess the threat which the Soviet Union poses is obviously a very difficult and imprecise activity. Attention has to be given not only to the massive Soviet military capability but also to the intentions (which can quickly change) and the actions of the Soviet leaders in the past as well as in recent times. While not accepting the more extreme interpretations which suggest that the Soviet Union is simply waiting for the chance to take over the west at the first opportunity, the history of Soviet domestic and foreign policy suggests that the west can do no other than take the threat posed by their military power seriously. The fundamental ideological differences, as well as the frequent clashes of national interest, between east and west, their impressive all-round military capability and their penchant for resolving crises by force, all indicate that no responsible western statesman could conclude that the USSR is definitely not a threat now and will not become one in the foreseeable future. To conclude that there was no threat and to get it wrong could well be disastrous.

From Britain's point of view the threat takes two main forms. First, there is the possibility of war arising from Soviet misjudgement as a result of a crisis, either inside or outside Europe. However cautious the Soviet Union may have been in the past, the fact remains that the inherent intractability of numerous conflicts between east and west in various world trouble-spots might at some time erupt into open hostilities. Such misjudgement might well be more, rather than less, likely if Britain and other western states were not adequately defended. Secondly, there is also the problem of 'Finlandisation'. One aspect of Soviet behaviour which does tend to stand out over the years is the sensitivity of the leadership towards neighbouring regimes who do not share the Soviet view of the world. Apart from outright intervention (in Hungary, Czechoslovakia and Afghanistan), Soviet regimes have also often employed more indirect intimidation to secure acceptance of the Kremlin's line on major policy issues. This phenomenon, known as 'Finlandisation' (after the nature of post-war Soviet–Finnish relations) could conceivably spread to Western Europe. The inability or reluctance of western states to defend themselves against the impressive military power of the Soviet Union might not bring outright invasion. But the recognition of inferiority coupled with pressure from the east might cause Western European states to adopt a policy of appeasement to the Soviet Union, giving in to any demands which might be made. Clearly life in Finland is not as bad as life in the Soviet Union or many other East European states but the limited independence of the Finns is obviously not one which western states would ideally choose. British defence policy is designed to prevent this state of affairs just as much as an outright invasion.

If one accepts that the Soviet Union does pose a threat to the UK, it does not of course necessarily follow that Britain should possess nuclear weapons as a result. It might be argued on strategic, political, economic and/or moral grounds that such a force is an inappropriate response and (unless one is a pacifist) that other forms of defence would suffice. Nevertheless, in the past at least, British governments of both right and left have argued that an independent British nuclear deterrent is an essential element in countering this perceived threat. Before we turn to some of the arguments put forward in defence of this view we need to spend a few moments considering the nature of the British nuclear force.

The British nuclear force

At the heart of British strategic doctrine is the threat to retaliate against an aggressor using both strategic and theatre nuclear weapons. In comparison with the superpowers, Britain's force is small but it does nevertheless possess the capability of inflicting unimaginable damage on an enemy, with the deaths of millions of people. The independent deterrent component of this force consists of four Polaris submarines, each with sixteen missiles (individually armed with three multiple reentry vehicle (MRV) warheads). Although only one submarine can be guaranteed to be on station at any time, the destructive power of a single warhead far exceeds that unleashed against Hiroshima and Nagasaki. Following the July 1980 and March 1982 agreements with the United States, Britain now intends to replace this force with Trident (D5) missiles in the early 1990s. The force once again is to consist of four submarines, each with sixteen missiles (this time with up to fourteen multiple independently targeted re-entry vehicle (MIRV) warheads, although the Defence Secretary has indicated that the British force will not employ anything like the maximum number of warheads). The extra range of this missile, together with the larger number and greater accuracy of the warheads, make it a significantly more powerful instrument than the present Polaris system.

In addition to this formidable strategic deterrent force, Britain also contributes a number of nuclear-capable systems to the overall NATO alliance deterrent. These include aircraft, like the ageing Vulcans and Buccaneers, as well as the newer Jaguars, Tornados and Sea Harriers, all of which are capable of a nuclear role. Nimrod maritime patrol aircraft and maritime helicopters also have the capability to deliver nuclear depth-bombs. In addition Britain has one regiment of Lance missiles and three regiments of dual-capable artillery based in Germany, equipped with American nuclear warheads (controlled by both Britain and the United States).

HOW CONVINCING ARE THE ARGUMENTS SUPPORTING A
BRITISH NUCLEAR FORCE?

Among the wide-ranging arguments used to justify this force the
following tend to be the most common:

1. A contribution to NATO and a 'second centre of decision'.
2. The trigger effect.
3. An insurance policy/a weapon of the last resort.
4. As a nucleus of a European deterrent.
5. Political utility.

A contribution to NATO and a 'second centre of decision'

Most government statements for the past twenty years or so have
stressed that the British force plays a crucial and indeed unique role
in enhancing the security of the North Atlantic Treaty Organisation
(NATO). It does this, according to official pronouncements, by providing 'a nuclear deterrent capability committed to the alliance yet
fully under the control of a European member'. In other words this
rationale emphasises that, although they would be mistaken, the Russians might come to believe in a crisis situation that the United
States would not be prepared to risk the nuclear destruction of the US
itself on behalf of the European members of the alliance, especially
at a time of strategic parity. If this were so, it is argued, the existence of
a separate nuclear force owned by a European state, capable of inflicting enormous damage, would cause the Soviet Union to think very
seriously indeed about aggression.

   The existence of the British force, so the argument runs, provides
extra insurance for the alliance. This is not simply because the force is
European and therefore more credible against a proposed attack on
West European states but also because it represents a 'second centre
of decision-making'. As such it helps to complicate the calculations of
a potential aggressor. In a crisis the Soviet Union would be forced to
contend with two sets of decision-makers rather than just one in the
United States. This would mean, according to the former Defence
Secretary, Francis Pym, in a speech to the House of Commons in
early 1980, that the risks to the Soviet Union would be 'inescapably
higher and the outcome of its actions much less certain'. It is precisely
this emphasis on uncertainty created in the minds of Soviet leaders by
a 'second centre of decision' which is often said to strengthen alliance

deterrence as a whole. The Soviet Union could never be certain that there would be no nuclear response and given the horrendous consequences of nuclear conflict they would be unlikely to risk an attack on Western Europe. This is sometimes called 'the certainty of uncertainty'.

It is perhaps not surprising that Britain should have adopted and constantly emphasised this argument for possessing a strategic nuclear force. As Lawrence Freedman has written elsewhere, 'the attraction of the argument lies as much in its diplomatic convenience as in the rigour of its strategic analysis'.[1] Such a defence of the force endorses both Britain's independent control and its commitment to strengthen the deterrent posture of the alliance as a whole. It also deals with the sensitivities of our European partners towards a possible weakening of the American nuclear guarantee in an age of strategic parity. Official statements emphasise that Britain's European allies recognise and welcome the British force as 'a central and unique component' of alliance strategy.

Apart from the diplomatic convenience, the argument does seem to have at least some strategic merit. A European response to aggression against European homelands is likely to carry greater credibility. It also seems reasonable to assume that the existence of different decision-makers in different states with important interests at stake would be likely to complicate the task of the Soviet leadership in deciding whether it could achieve its objectives at the least possible cost and risk to itself. Uncertainty in not being able to predict the outcome of one's actions in a potentially nuclear environment must have an inhibiting affect. In some respects also the existence of a second centre of decision actually makes the prospects of a response more likely from the Soviet point of view.

The argument, however, is not without flaws. It must be admitted that in comparison with the American strategic arsenal the British contribution to the alliance (at least in percentage terms) is negligible. A British decision to abandon its strategic nuclear weapons therefore would be unlikely to weaken Western capability overall in any significant way.

There must also be a question mark over the stress placed on the European nature of the British force. It could be argued quite legitimately that if the United States decided to stay out of a confrontation in Europe to save its cities from nuclear devastation, the same might also be true of Britain. Or to use the reasoning behind official government statements themselves, if the Soviet Union came to the conclusion that the United States might not respond with nuclear weapons on behalf of Europe, it might also conclude the same about Britain given Britain's traditional and continuing ambivalence towards the continent. Indeed given the consequences for Britain of a nuclear exchange it might seem perfectly reasonable to assume that it would be very unlikely indeed to unleash its nuclear forces in any circumstances other than a direct threat to the British mainland.

Another problem is the emphasis which the 'second centre of decision' argument places on the role of uncertainty in deterrence. It was argued above that complicating Soviet decision-making and thereby creating extra uncertainty in the minds of Soviet leaders might be likely to inhibit risky Soviet behaviour. However, there is inevitably a worry about basing one's security, especially in the nuclear age, on the notion of uncertainty. This may seem a rather flimsy, unsatisfactory and imprecise notion upon which to base strategic planning. Deterrence is usually thought to be enhanced by increasing the certainty of response rather than emphasising uncertainty. Indeed the more automatic the commitment the more effective the deterrent is likely to be. It would seem a curious argument, therefore, that creating uncertainty contributes to deterrence. The government might do better to stress the fact that an additional nuclear power in the alliance increases the likelihood of response rather than emphasising the benefits of uncertainty.

Overall it would seem difficult to disprove the proposition that Britain's contribution to the alliance and the complication it causes for Soviet planners is of value in strengthening the western deterrent. It must be said, however, as we have argued, that the arguments supporting this view do not appear to be wholly satisfactory. Certainly to many observers they provide a far from convincing justification for the British strategic deterrent.

The trigger effect

Another argument often put forward in favour of the independent deterrent is that it could be used to trigger the use of the much bigger American nuclear arsenal. If the American government were hesitant in a crisis, or both superpowers agreed to try to limit a conflict to Europe, the British deterrent could be used as a catalyst to force the American hand. Those who support this justification claim that the Soviet leaders would not be able to distinguish between British and American missiles and given the mutual suspicion of any European confrontation they would inevitably respond to any nuclear attack by striking the US itself. In turn the United States would be forced to respond.

Such an argument has a certain superficial attraction. Technically it probably would be very difficult for the Soviet Union to differentiate between missiles fired from British or American submarines (although the new British Chevaline warhead is said to have a rather distinctive configuration). The question is whether the United States would allow itself to be dragged, against its wishes, into such a conflict. There is also a serious doubt whether such a reckless use of its missiles would be in the UK's best interests. Given the inevitable consequences to Britain of Polaris or Trident missiles being fired, there would seem to be a much greater incentive to hold back the process of escalation for as long as possible rather than to accelerate it. It is for this reason in particular that the implicit threat to utilise the British force to implicate the US is not likely to be taken very seriously by Soviet leaders. As such it cannot be said to contribute very much to the credibility of British deterrence.

Insurance policy/weapon of the last resort

In recent years the argument heard more and more often in defence of a strategic nuclear capability is that it provides an insurance policy for an uncertain future. As a result of strategic parity between the United States and the USSR and the increased questioning of the American nuclear guarantee, it is frequently argued that, in a dangerous world, Britain must have ultimate control over its own national security. The great fear often expressed (although only rarely by government officials in public) is that Britain might at some point in the future have to stand alone. In such circumstances, difficult as they may be to foresee, nuclear weapons would be reassuring and might be decisive in preserving British identity, values and independence. Echoing Gaullist sentiments, a 1975 House of Commons Expenditure Committee Report argued that:

> In the last resort, if the Alliance was to collapse, the possession of an independent strategic weapon provides the UK with a means of preserving national security by deterring large-scale conventional or nuclear attack or countering blackmail.[2]

According to ex-Secretary of State for Defence, Mr Nott, no other form of military power would be capable of dealing with nuclear blackmail or the threat of a large-scale conventional or nuclear devastation if Britain did ever find itself alone.

Those who question this argument usually do so on two main grounds. First, that the circumstances in which Britain might have to act on its own are so inconceivable as to be not worth planning for. Second, that even if one could conceive of such a possibility, the British deterrent alone is not credible against the might of the Soviet Union.

It is indeed difficult to imagine the precise circumstances in which independent action of this kind against the Soviet Union would become necessary. Such a situation presumably could only come about if the United States had disassociated itself from the defence of Western Europe and NATO had disintegrated. Or alternatively, Britain might have opted for a policy of isolationism in an increasingly anarchic international system, basing its independence on the threat of nuclear retaliation against any threats to the integrity of the nation. Neither scenario is particularly likely but certainly the former cannot be as easily dismissed as some writers tend to do.

The basic question here is whether remote contingencies should be catered for. Remote contingencies do have to be confronted from time to time, as the recent Falklands crisis has demonstrated. If the consequences of not paying the premium for such insurance might be high (as it would be if Britain ever found itself alone) then there would seem to be a strong case for prudence in defence decision-making.

The second criticism is that even if such circumstances are imaginable, the British nuclear force is unlikely to be effective in deterring Soviet action. Indeed its use might well bring in retaliation the total destruction of the British way of life. Behind this particular argument there often lies the belief that Britain's force could not play a credible independent role because it still remains dependent on the United States. Without US support Britain would be deprived of the vast range of technical and information assistance to which it has access at present: assistance with intelligence, targetting, navigation and communications (and in the longer term, testing, nuclear materials and spare parts). Important as this American help is, it seems highly unlikely that it is crucial to the effective functioning of the British force. The Defence Secretary, John Nott, went out of his way to tell the House of Commons on March 30 1982 that 'Britain was in no way dependent on the United States for communications, targetting or any other matter of day-to-day operation of the force.' Clearly, however, the longer the estrangement between the two countries, the more Britain would have to compensate from its own sources or new defence partnerships for the wide range of assistance now received from the US.

There is an even more telling argument against the credibility of a British threat to launch missiles against the Soviet Union. British leaders would know that although their force could wreak truly enormous damage on the Soviet Union, Britain's own cities and military installations could be obliterated in a Soviet nuclear attack. Such knowledge of unequal destructive power and unequal consequences, so it is often argued, means that no sane British Prime Minister would ever initiate such an attack and that Soviet leaders would be likely to believe that they would not. Such an argument has been authoritatively developed by Lord Carver who ended a long and distinguished career in the British Army as the Chief of the Defence Staff. In a much quoted speech in the House of Lords in December 1979 he claimed that:

> Over the years the arguments have shifted and I have read them all; but in that time I have never heard or read a scenario which I would consider it right or reasonable for the Prime Minister or Government of this country to order the firing of our independent strategic force at a time when the Americans were not preapred to fire theirs – certainly not before Russian nuclear weapons had landed in this country. And again, if they had already landed, would it be right and reasonable? All it would do would be to invite further retaliation.

Lord Carver was suggesting that the British nuclear deterrent lacked credibility even as a last-resort threat to prevent Soviet nuclear blackmail or a direct attack on Britain itself. He also quite rightly points to the very real dangers to Britain of a strategy of nuclear deterrence. This clearly is a powerful critique from a man who spent over twenty-one years dealing with issues of national security from the inside.

Such a viewpoint, even if expressed by such a prominent military figure, is not decisive. There are plenty of other high-ranking military men and scientific officials in retirement whose judgement is somewhat different. Despite major criticisms of NATO nuclear strategy, Lord Zuckerman, who as Chief Scientific Adviser to the Ministry of

Defence and to various Prime Ministers for thirteen years, had access to much the same level of defence planning as Lord Carver, is one who believes that Britain should not disarm unilaterally.

Lord Carver's case is that it would be irrational for Britain to respond in nuclear terms to a Soviet attack. Ironically perhaps, many unilateralists believe that in the emotional atmosphere of war Britain might well respond, irrational as that action would be. It is for this very reason that they seek to get rid of the British nuclear force. What matters, of course, is what the Soviet leaders' perception would be. Would the Soviet leaders in 'a situation without precedent and of unique peril' be likely to believe that the British just might fire their missiles? Could the Soviet leadership ever discount the possibility that faced with a threat to a civilisation built up so proudly over many generations, and defended with such obstinate vigour in the past, Britain might respond? The answer, of course, is that we do not know. It does, however, seem likely that given the horrendous damage that even the small British nuclear capability could inflict on an adversary the possibilities of irrational behaviour in exceptional international circumstances in defence of vital interests could not be ruled out altogether by Soviet leaders planning to blackmail or attack Britain. Even a 5 per cent chance of British retaliation might well be enough to deter them.

Despite the reservations, then, it seems that the last resort argument is probably the most persuasive of those so far discussed. As its critics argue, there are some problems in imagining the precise circumstances in which a British force might be used. There is also a question mark over the credibility of the force in any confrontation with the Soviet Union. Certainly any such confrontation would bring very grave dangers to Britain. On the other hand, it must also be said that no one can predict with confidence that such circumstances will never arise in the future. Neither is it possible to conclude that a last-resort weapon of such destructive power would not inhibit the behaviour of potential aggressors. Common sense seems to suggest that it would.

In many respects the question of whether Britain should have strategic nuclear weapons comes down to a balance of risks. There are, however, a number of further points we need to consider before a final assessment can be made on whether, overall, the balance of argument is in favour or against the possession of such a force.

The nucleus of a European deterrent

The previous argument was based largely on the uncertainties of international relations in the future. There is also an argument which suggests that at some point in the years ahead Europe will achieve a level of political integration which forces states to reconsider proposals for a European defence community and perhaps a nuclear deterrent system of its own. Seen from this point of view it would be foolish for the UK to opt out of the nuclear business now when by maintaining its capability it could provide, or contribute to, the nucleus of a future European defence system.

Those who advocate this line suggest that a European force could come about in a number of different ways and that such a force would have various advantages over a purely independent British capability. Such a force could conceivably be achieved by Britain and France pooling their expertise and operating a joint Anglo-French deterrent force on behalf of Europe. Alternatively, it might be possible to develop a wider European defence organisation (on the lines of the European Defence Community (EDC) in the early 1950s) in which the technological know-how of all the members, including West Germany and Italy, as well as Britain and France, was shared.

Either development could be advantageous for Britain. In political terms, it would demonstrate Britain's firm commitment to Europe. In economic terms, it would enable Britain to share the heavy costs of maintaining up-to-date technology with our wealthier European allies. And in strategic terms, it would provide a deterrent system backed by the community as a whole and more formidable than anything Britain could provide by itself.

Appealing as either 'European solution' might appear, they do, however, present a number of major difficulties. Negotiations between Britain and France on some form of nuclear cooperation have taken place on numerous occasions since the late 1950s. They have always foundered, however, on the twin problems of French independence and Britain's treaty obligations to the United States not to pass on nuclear information to third parties without their consent. There is also a question mark over whether a future Anglo-French nuclear guarantee would be any more effective to the rest of Europe than the present American guarantee. The same kind of pressures which threaten to undermine the latter would be likely to undermine the former.

A European deterrent is also problematical politically. As yet there is little sign that Europe will achieve the kind of political integration necessary to make a European defence organisation workable. There are also the additional political problems of involving Germany in any European nuclear force. Under the terms of the Paris agreements of 1954, which preceded the controlled rearmament of West Germany, a stipulation was included that the Federal Republic of Germany (FRG) would not develop nuclear weapons. This restriction remains a sensitive issue in east–west relations, in the western alliance and not least within West Germany itself.

In addition to these problems a European nuclear force representing the EEC members might not be acceptable to all members of the Community. Ireland in particular, and perhaps Holland as well, would find it difficult to support such a policy. Linked to this is the inevitable difficulty of matching any European system with the North Atlantic Treaty Organisation. Quite apart from the fact that such a force might itself weaken the American resolve to defend Western Europe, not all EEC members are members of NATO. The result would be an alliance within an alliance, with some members in both alliances and some in only one.

Thus some kind of European force would seem to require important political changes which have yet to appear on the horizon. For some the potential advantages of such a force suggest that Britain should retain its own capability and work towards the establishment of a European deterrent system as an ultimate objective. For others such a force is both unattainable and undesirable.

The political utility

One reason often put forward for an independent deterrent, at least in the past, has been that it confers a degree of international prestige and status. It has sometimes been suggested that such a capability demonstrates technological excellence and puts the possessor in a different league to other non-nuclear powers. In Britain's case, it has also been said to confer special influence in the United States and an important say in arms control negotiations between east and west.

Status and prestige in international politics are obviously difficult things to measure. It may well be that nuclear weapons do help to confer these attributes but clearly they are not in themselves sufficient to confer great power status. A number of states, including Germany and Japan, because of their economic success and Britain's relative economic decline, would seem to be higher up the international league table. It could perhaps be argued that Britain's decline as a world power might have been even more precipitate had it not maintained this major symbol of power throughout the post-war period. Those opposed to the retention of nuclear weapons would disagree. Many writers, on the left in particular, argue that the attempt to stay at the forefront of the nuclear field has drained important resources away from the economy and prevented Britain from coming to terms with its true position as a declining medium-range power. Nuclear weapons have helped to create an illusion of great power status which has often resulted in Britain spending too much on defence generally and has helped to deflect successive governments from the urgent task of restructuring and revitalising an ailing economy. Whether or not this is so, status, real or imagined, is hardly a major reason for possessing such weapons.

There is clearly also a difficulty in assessing how much influence nuclear weapons confer. It may well be that their possession has helped Britain to maintain the 'special relationship' with the United States and thereby a degree of influence in Washington. Britain has probably also been able to play an influential role in the Nuclear Planning Group in NATO, as the only European nuclear power in that forum. And in the past at least (although Britain was not involved in SALT) the fact that Britain has been an important nuclear power has helped it to make an important contribution to arms control negotiations between east and west. In all of these cases nuclear weapons probably have brought *some* political benefits to Britain. However, it would be hard to conclude from such examples as these that nuclear weapons have been a major source of political power for Britain in the past.

On the other hand it must also be admitted that nuclear weapons have not really been a source of great political embarrassment to Britain either. The UK has been in the nuclear business from the start and has not had to face the difficulties of countries like France and China in developing and building up their nuclear weapons programme when the weight of world opinion has been opposed to nuclear proliferation. Neither has it been forced to operate in a clandestine way to try to produce nuclear weapons (like South Africa, Israel, Argentina and a number of others). In this sense, then, although nuclear weapons may not have produced great political benefits they have not generated undue political costs either.

An interesting contemporary example of the difficulty of evaluating the political utility of nuclear weapons as an instrument of foreign policy can be seen from the Falklands crisis of spring 1982. On the one hand a strong case can be made that Britain's nuclear weapons were irrelevant in the confrontation between Britain and Argentina. The fact that Britain possessed such weapons clearly did not deter an Argentinian invasion and occupation of the Falkland islands. The Argentinian junta came to the conclusion that despite the possession of this massive military potential Britain would not use or threaten to use such weapons to compel the Argentinian armed forces to withdraw.

There is, however, another point of view worthy of consideration. If Argentina had possessed nuclear weapons would Britain have sent the task force to the South Atlantic? The answer is probably not, and certainly not, if the Argentinian junta had possessed nuclear weapons and Britain had not. The absence of nuclear weapons on one side and their possession by the other therefore would seem to have at least some bearing on a dispute of this kind. One should obviously be careful about drawing lessons from a unique crisis and especially from hypothetical circumstances. In a world in which the proliferation of nuclear weapons is likely to increase, however, the attempt to use nuclear blackmail is also likely to be greater. In such circumstances it seems fair to say that the lack of nuclear weapons could well seriously inhibit British options in defence of its interests.

Whether on balance all this adds up to a strong political case for nuclear weapons is, however, perhaps doubtful. The arguments on both sides suggest that the case is marginal. Certainly the political rationales only provide supplementary support, if at all, and not a major justification for a British independent deterrent.

So far we have considered a number of strategic and political arguments which we have attempted to suggest are finely balanced. There are two further sets of arguments, one moral and one economic, which may tilt the balance of argument one way or the other.

IS THE MORAL ARGUMENT DECISIVE?

The argument which is, in some ways, the most difficult for supporters of a British force to deal with is the moral objection to weapons of mass destruction. At the root of many people's opposition to an independent deterrent, and more powerful than all the other arguments, is the conviction that there can be no conceivable justification for launching such horrific weapons or, indeed, for relying on a strategy which threatens to use such weapons. To those who provide a moral objection to nuclear weapons, the level of instantaneous destruction, the lingering effects of radiation and the longer-term genetic complications associated with the use of thermonuclear weapons, put such weapons in a category all of their own. For many contemporary critics of the government's nuclear defence policy, no objective can possibly justify the use of such weapons. For many of those who hold such convictions the conclusion is inevitable: Britain must unilaterally disarm and disassociate itself from any strategy of nuclear deterrence. It is sometimes conceded that the consequences of such action might increase the possibilities of conventional war and ultimately perhaps the occupation of Britain by a foreign power. This would be undesirable, it is argued, but preferable to the present reliance on nuclear weapons. To those who hold this 'absolutist' view, then, the moral argument is decisive.

There are, however, more relative views of morality which in different ways and in varying degrees take issue with this absolutist line. Some argue, for example, that although the use of nuclear weapons is morally repugnant and can never be justified, a strategy which *threatens* their use may be morally acceptable. In this sense nuclear deterrence is acceptable in moral terms if such a policy helps to achieve certain objectives like peace and security. What matters, according to this view, are the consequences. This is sometimes described as the 'consequentialist' moral viewpoint. But if deterrence broke down (and there can be no certain guarantee that it will not) and nuclear weapons are used, such action because of the consequences inevitably must be regarded as immoral. According to this view, therefore, nuclear deterrence is acceptable until it breaks down. The implication is that states can justifiably bluff with nuclear weapons but if that bluff is ever called they should give in or at least refrain from doing what they have previously threatened they would do. This may well be a reasonable pragmatic strategy but can it be defended on moral grounds? To the 'absolutist', the answer is no. To threaten to use nuclear weapons is just as bad as actually to use them. There is, however, the question of intention which must be borne in mind. Professor Hedley Bull has written that:

All policies of nuclear deterrence, unilateral or bilateral are morally disreputable. The deliberate slaughtering of millions of innocent people for whatever reason is wicked. So is threatening to do so, if that means that we actually intend to carry out the threat (as according to Western and Soviet doctrines, we do).[3]

Defenders of the 'consequentialist' viewpoint would respond to this view by saying that although nuclear deterrence does threaten to kill innocent people, it is justifiable in moral terms if there is no intention actually to carry out your threat.

Despite the obvious practical difficulties (of deterrence without the will to back it up) this view cannot be wholly dismissed on moral grounds. There is a respectable position in moral thinking which accepts that if the end result is for the greater good then the means to achieve that good are morally acceptable. To shoot a terrorist who threatens to blow up his hostages would be morally justifiable in these terms. Likewise it is argued by some nuclear deterrence theorists and supporters of the British nuclear force that if the threat to use British nuclear weapons against an aggressor helps to keep the peace (and it does *seem* to have done this in the past) then such an objective cannot be described as immoral. Some would say this was so regardless of the intention because peace and independence are in themselves high moral values. On this basis, a unilateralist position may be deemed much less morally acceptable because the end result may well be a less stable international situation in which there is a greater likelihood of world war (even if war remains conventional) with the loss of millions of lives.

Another relativist position adopted by some who accept the theory of nuclear deterrence is that the use of nuclear weapons and indeed even the threat to use them *is* morally wrong but that weakening 'nuclear deterrence to the point of jeopardising our security' is also morally objectionable. Such an argument claims that there is a *moral dilemma* which is inescapable and insoluble: there are no courses of action which are free of moral difficulty. In such circumstances the main objectives of security policy should be to keep the peace and preserve the values of society. The least unsatisfactory way of doing this, it is argued, is through a policy of nuclear deterrence supplemented by arms control measures (see Chapter 2). Such a policy then accepts that nuclear deterrence involves wickedness (which should not be forgotten) but argues that deficient as such strategy probably is, there seems little alternative at present if peace and security are to be secured.

These more complicated views of morality are those with which the authors have most sympathy. We accept that others may hold the kind of alternative absolutist moral position described above and that, to them, the simple moral arguments are the most important in any discussion of British nuclear weapons. It must be said that the relativist views of morality held by the authors do not in themselves indicate that Britain should necessarily possess nuclear weapons but simply that moral considerations, important as they are, are not necessarily decisive or so clear-cut as they often seem.

CAN BRITAIN AFFORD NUCLEAR WEAPONS?

In the current debate about the Trident force as a replacement for Polaris, the question of the costs involved has loomed large. Even for many people who have been prepared to go along with the British deterrent force in the past, the expenditure of somewhere in the region of £7500 million spread over roughly fifteen years, is simply too much. For them it is the economic argument that is decisive in their opposition to the new programme.

Those who worry about the costs involved can be divided into a number of different groups. The important point with all of these groups is not the total amount of money involved – very large as this undoubtedly is – but the opportunity costs: that is, those things which have to be foregone by spending such resources on nuclear weapons.

There are those, particularly on the left, who would like to see this money spent solely on the civilian economy. In their criticisms they point to the number of hospital beds, kidney machines, schools, roads, etc. which could be provided if the money to be spent on nuclear weapons was diverted to other things. They also point to the lost investment opportunities which result from such expenditure. Clearly these are powerful arguments at a time of such high unemployment in Britain, when it is government policy deliberately to cut back on major public expenditure. 'Jobs not bombs' makes a strong emotional slogan at such times.

Seen from this angle, it is very much a question of government priorities. The government, so the argument runs, has got its priorities wrong. Given the state of the British economy and all of the social problems facing the country it simply does not make sense to purchase one of the most expensive weapons systems in the world.

The question of priorities is also at the heart of the opposition of another group. There are, those, some within the defence establishment itself, who argue that money spent on Trident is money which cannot be spent on other conventional weapons. This very powerful lobby believes that Britain's conventional forces will inevitably suffer as a result of the decision to purchase Trident. Indeed they argue that this process has already begun with Mr Nott's Defence Review of June 1981, when cuts were announced, particularly in Britain's surface naval forces. They also point to the high percentages of research and development and of the equipment budget (16 per cent and 10 per cent respectively) to be taken up by the new nuclear weapons programme. Those who take this line suggest that it is very dangerous for Britain's security both in the NATO context (by helping to lower the nuclear threshold) and outside, to run down the nation's conventional forces. As the Falkland crisis demonstrated, it is argued, these are precisely the kinds of forces which are most needed.

Such arguments are not necessarily opposed to nuclear weapons per se, but simply to the costs involved. Indeed some of those who argue along these lines suggest that although Trident might be too expensive, another cheaper deterrent might be acceptable. This is an argument we will return to later.

Supporters of the Polaris and Trident programmes reject the criticism that Britain cannot afford such weapons. They point to the fact that over the past twenty-five years governments of both parties have spent between 2 and 10 per cent of the defence budget on strategic nuclear weapons; that the present Polaris programme absorbs about 1.5–2 per cent of the defence budget; and that Trident will take up only slightly more (about 3 per cent p.a. on average) over the fifteen or twenty years it takes to build it. This, they argue, is hardly excessive in terms of the total defence expenditure.

In response to the argument that the money could be better spent on other things, government officials argue that the 'threat' to schools, roads and hospitals have to be set against the threats to the nation's security. At issue therefore is not the stark choice between 'guns or butter' but how many (and what sort) of guns versus how much butter. In such an assessment, it is argued, that given that security is an important priority, money spent on Trident is particularly cost-effective. As Mr Nott told the House of Commons on 12 March 1982, 'no other use of our resources could possibly contribute as much to our security and the deterrent strength of NATO as a whole'. In other words, in the view of the Secretary of State for Defence, spending this money on *extra* tanks, planes, ships or missiles would not make us qualitatively stronger. Trident provides a unique and vital dimension to British defence policy.

It is also argued that although 'money spent on Trident is not money spent elsewhere', the government through continuing to spend an extra 3 per cent p.a. on defence (in line with its NATO commitment) intends to go on improving Britain's conventional forces in the future. The Ministry of Defence argues that the 1981 Defence Review was intended to reshape, in a more effective way, the nation's defence effort, making use of new technology, rather than to weaken defence.

These arguments about cost are difficult to evaluate. Clearly the nation can afford nuclear weapons if it wishes. Indeed the scale of the expenditure on Trident does seem to have been exaggerated by its opponents. It may well be the most cost-effective system available. It is nevertheless true that the opportunity costs, particularly in other areas of defence, are important considerations. With the continuing problem of the British economy and high levels of defence inflation (despite the government commitment to 3 per cent increase in defence expenditure through to 1986) there must be a serious question mark over whether the nation's conventional forces will be maintained or improved alongside the expenditure on Trident. This would probably be true too in some respects of any other viable alternative replacement for the present Polaris force.

SUMMARY

We suggested earlier that the various strategic and political arguments concerning the possession by Britain of an independent strategic nuclear deterrent were reasonably finely balanced. A survey of the moral and economic arguments does not suggest to us that there is any major reason for changing this assessment. During our discussion of the strategic and moral arguments we suggested that there were difficulties and dangers with nuclear deterrence. The question which remains to be considered is whether there are alternative defence policies which would provide Britain with more security than the present reliance on nuclear weapons. If there are it would seem sensible to give up the force. If not, the conclusion might be that we should live with what we have unless, and until, a suitable alternative can be found. Before tackling this question it might be appropriate to spend some time considering the CND movement in Britain which advocates strongly that there are viable non-nuclear alternatives which should be adopted.

WHY HAS THERE BEEN A RESURGENCE OF CND?

After the halcyon days of the Campaign for Nuclear Disarmament at the end of the 1950s and early 1960s, the movement underwent a significant decline in the remainder of the 1960s and 1970s. Its membership fell away and it was largely irrelevant as a pressure group. One of the most interesting features of the present nuclear debate is the rekindling of the CND movement and the dramatic resurgence of popular support reflected in rapidly increasing membership and the size of anti-nuclear demonstrations in the early 1980s. In this respect the CND is part of the wider peace movement which has emerged all over Western Europe and the British organisation itself has established close links with the European Nuclear Disarmament (END) movement.

The reasons for this revitalisation of the campaign are not difficult to find. The late 1970s and early 1980s witnessed a significant deterioration of east–west relations, with the Soviet invasion of Afghanistan, the failure of the Carter administration to seek the ratification of the SALT 2 treaty, the inauguration of a new President in the US committed to a tougher line and major increases in defence spending, and Soviet reaction to the Polish crisis. At the same time weapons modernisation programmes, with the focus on the threat from Soviet SS-20 missiles, the proposed American cruise and Pershing missile deployments in Western Europe, the neutron bomb saga, talk of limited nuclear war and finally Britain's decision to replace Polaris with Trident, all helped to create a genuine concern amongst ordinary people that war was a distinct possibility. At this time of inevitable public concern, the existing CND and the new END movements were led by enthusiastic and charismatic individuals determined not to make the mistakes of the 1950s. Certainly a much greater attempt has been made by these movements this time to avoid damaging personality clashes at the top, to retain unity and also to enter into a higher-level debate and take on the defence studies community on its own terms. It must also be said that their cause was assisted by the slow and somewhat ineffective way in which the authorities attempted to get their message across to the public.

Another contributory factor was the record of relative failure of previous multilateral arms control negotiations. (See Chapter 2.) The American failure to ratify SALT 2 helped to highlight the fact that after twenty years of negotiation between east and west the arms race was still continuing at a frightening pace. Not surprisingly there was a

growth in support for the CND message that multilateralism had
failed and the unilateralist approach was the only alternative to a
continuation of the arms race and – inevitably – nuclear war. The
message was emotionally appealing. CND seemed to many to offer
the only way out.

WHAT DOES CND STAND FOR?

According to most CND publications, the campaign has five main
objectives:

1. No Trident submarines to replace Polaris.
2. No cruise missiles on British territory.
3. No other nuclear weapons on British soil or in British waters.
4. No bases for British or American nuclear weapons.
5. A cut in arms spending.

These five objectives are regarded as immediate aims with the ultimate objective being general and complete disarmament. The CND
accepts that the Americans and the Russians are unlikely to forsake
their nuclear weapons 'for some years ahead' and they also admit that
there is no *guarantee* that other countries would follow Britain's lead.
They do, however, claim that because of the UK's close language,
trade, diplomatic and historical relations with many countries
throughout the world, unilateral action by Britain 'would have greater effect than that of any other country except the two superpowers'.
They also argue that the alternative to unilateralism is an increase in
the competitive arms race which 'is *certain* to bring disaster, probably
sooner rather than later'. The reasons put forward in support of CND
aims usually involve a combination of survival, morality and finance.
'New missiles increase the dangers for Britain'; 'the use of nuclear
bombs means causing the death of millions of men, women and children'; and 'the money would be better spent on housing, health,
education, pensions and social services'.

Appealing as these arguments are they are not without serious
criticism. In particular the premise that British unilateral action
would have a profound effect on the policies of other states would
seem to be little more than wishful thinking. States decide to acquire
nuclear weapons or not for a variety of complex reasons, the most
important of which involve assessments of the capabilities of their

potential adversaries and their own regional security. It is highly unlikely that British renunciation would have any impact whatsoever upon the thinking of the governments of India, Pakistan, Israel, South Africa or Brazil. Other considerations are far more important. There is also the damaging argument presented by CND supporters that nuclear war is inevitable if present policies are pursued. Nothing is inevitable, only more or less likely. Stating that something is inevitable may make the occurrence more likely. Nuclear weapons and the policies of deterrence have been around for a long time without global exchanges taking place. Those who argue that the world is now more dangerous than ever before as a result of technological changes and difficulties in east–west relations would do well to consider the instability of the strategic balance at the height of the cold war in the late 1950s and early 1960s. There is clearly no room for complacency but neither should we succumb to the fatalistic determinism of the CND message.

HOW POPULAR IS CND?

Despite this dramatic and public resurgence of the campaign in recent years the evidence from the opinion polls taken between September 1980 and November 1981 is somewhat ambiguous. On the specific issue of Trident, which helped to spark off the new campaign, public support for the new missile (according to a Marplan poll) declined from 44 per cent in September 1980 to 32 per cent in April 1981. One might assume from this that public support for unilateralism was well in excess of 50 per cent. In fact this is not the case. In the twelve months from September 1980 support for unilateral renunciation of nuclear weapons varied between 20 per cent and 34 per cent. In a Gallup poll taken in November 1981 well over half those interviewed still felt that it would be a mistake for Britain to give up its nuclear weapons if other countries did not follow suit. One obviously has to be careful about interpreting the meaning of such polls. What this might indicate, however, is that the majority of the British public, at least at present, are in favour of some form of multilateral rather than unilateral disarmament but that until this can be achieved, some alternative (perhaps cheaper) nuclear deterrent to Trident should be maintained.

DOES BRITAIN HAVE ANY ALTERNATIVE NON-NUCLEAR DEFENCE OPTIONS?

One of the ways in which CND and others opposed to the independent deterrent are trying to influence public opinion is by putting forward alternative non-nuclear defence policies. Within the CND movement there is wide agreement, as we have seen, that Britain should not possess nuclear weapons of any kind: neither long-range strategic nor intermediate-range theatre weapons. There is less widespread consensus on what kind of alternative defence policy Britain should adopt. The movement runs into difficulties because some of its members are pacifists while others are not. The only alternative acceptable to some is purely passive resistance; while others are prepared to go for almost any form of defence which does not involve nuclear weapons. Amongst the latter group there is also considerable disagreement over whether Britain should remain in NATO, which is, after all, a nuclear alliance. Those who support continued membership of NATO point to countries like Canada, Norway and Denmark as three states which combine participation in alliance defence with a refusal to allow nuclear weapons to be stationed on their territory (at least in peacetime). Those who oppose NATO membership argue that Britain should have nothing to do with any organisation which threatens to use nuclear weapons, even if Britain does not participate itself in the actual use of these weapons.

The CND movement has been unable to put forward a single set of widely supported positive alternatives to the present defence policy. Yet it is worth spending a few moments looking at some of the wide variety of the different proposals suggested.

NON-NUCLEAR CONVENTIONAL DEFENCE WITHIN NATO

One idea considered by the Labour Party is that Britain should renounce the use of all nuclear weapons, ask the United States to withdraw its nuclear weapons from US bases in Britain, and provide only conventional forces for the alliance. To make this change more palatable to its NATO partners, Britain might even increase its conventional contribution to make up for withdrawing its nuclear forces and facilities.

There are several ways in which this new emphasis on conventional weapons might be achieved. It might be done either within the context of the present weapons mix and deployment patterns or through the adoption of radically new weapons mixes (utilising new anti-aircraft and anti-tank missile technology, etc.) and new force deployments on the continent. There are also a number of changes which Britain might adopt in terms of different contributions to alliance land, sea and air forces. Britain might, for example, play a bigger role in naval and air operations and contribute relatively less to the central front as the naval lobby in Britain currently argues. On the other hand, given the political significance of the British Army of the Rhine (BAOR), Britain might increase its ground forces in Europe (perhaps through conscription) and maintain its present naval and air deployments.

A quite convincing case can be made for concentrating on conventional forces. At present NATO's strategy of flexible response relies upon a spectrum of conventional, theatre nuclear and strategic options to deter the Soviet Union. If deterrence were to break down, given the superiority of the Soviet Union at the conventional level, NATO would probably be forced to use nuclear weapons first. There are many high-ranking military and scientific figures in the west, including the late Lord Mountbatten and Lord Zuckerman, who argue that as soon as the first nuclear weapon is used the conflict will almost certainly escalate. Such a process is perhaps not *inevitable* because both sides will clearly have an incentive to keep the conflict limited. However, the chances are high that a thermonuclear strategic exchange would result. The present authors themselves have very little faith in notions of limited nuclear war-fighting.

This being the case, an attempt by Britain to improve NATO's conventional defences and in so doing to persuade its allies to do the same would help to raise the nuclear threshold. Deterrence would be enhanced (in the sense that a western conventional response would be more likely to deter than a nuclear response) and NATO strategy would appear less immediately dangerous than the present almost automatic reliance on nuclear weapons.

Despite its appeal, this approach is not without serious flaws. One would be the difficulties it would cause in relations with the United States. Unilateral disarmament and the closing down of American nuclear bases, at a time when Soviet military capability (both nuclear and conventional) is increasing, would almost certainly have an adverse effect on US public opinion, Congress and on the US administration. Even with British conventional rearmament, American opinion would be likely to see such a move as a distinct weakening of alliance capability and a serious obstruction to America's ability to respond across the board to Soviet aggression. As far as alliance strategy is concerned, Britain – now in possession of its own nuclear weapons – cannot be compared with Canada, Norway or Denmark. Such an attempt to opt out of nuclear responsibility might cause a significant reappraisal of the US commitment to the defence of Western Europe (comparable to attempts by Senator Mansfield in the 1960s to reduce American forces on the European continent). If the American government did decide to withdraw a proportion or all of its conventional forces in Europe there could be no meaningful conventional response to the Soviet Union and the alliance would be in danger of falling apart.

American and European opinion also would be likely to stress the hypocrisy of such a British move. What, in effect, the UK would be saying to the alliance is that it is quite prepared to shelter under the nuclear umbrella of the United States and be part of an alliance which uses nuclear weapons against invading Soviet forces, but it wants nothing to do with such weapons itself. It is difficult to believe that such a posture has any more moral merit than the present policy.

There are those, however, who are prepared to accept such hypocrisy in the belief that Britain would then cease to be a nuclear target for the Soviet Union. Their assumption is that if there are no nuclear systems operating from British territory the Soviet Union will have less incentive in a war to use nuclear weapons against Britain. There is obviously something in this argument. It does, however, tend to ignore the problem of nuclear blackmail and the ambiguity in Soviet writings about the use of nuclear weapons in war. Although Soviet writers emphasise that there can be no such thing as a limited nuclear exchange they do stress the efficacy of nuclear weapons in a war-fighting role. In any conflict with the Soviet Union there would clearly be numerous important military targets in Britain, particularly if it remained the major reinforcement base for American troops, equipment and supplies. There are also the range of vital communications and intelligence facilities which would provide very tempting nuclear targets for the Russian leaders. It is hard to believe that in a conflict in Europe, in which nuclear weapons might well be used, Britain would remain a nuclear-free sanctuary.

NON-NUCLEAR DEFENCE OUTSIDE NATO

For some of these reasons at least, many CND supporters believe that the only acceptable alternative for Britain is to try to defend itself as best it can outside the alliance framework. In essence this would involve the adoption of a neutralist position, an 'opting out' of the east–west struggle.

Britain might simply withdraw its forces from the continent and from the alliance generally and concentrate them in the defence of Britain itself. Under such a scheme the Army and RAF would be based solely in the UK. They would be equipped and deployed purely to defend British territory. The Navy would cease to concentrate on the eastern Atlantic and its other NATO roles and would involve itself primarily in the coastal defence of the UK (with the kinds of ships required for such defence). The objective would be to make the price of an invasion of Britain too high for a potential aggressor. The UK, it is argued, would be more secure anyway because it would be outside the great power blocs and their conflicts.

A variation of this proposal would be for Britain to run down its conventional forces and to plan for guerrilla-style civilian resistance to any aggressor. Once again the objective would be to threaten constantly to harass any invading or occupying force and make life unbearable for them. Such a threat (as in the case of Yugoslavia), it is sometimes argued, would be a powerful deterrent.

A similar, although essentially pacifist plan, would be for passive resistance to occupying forces. The idea would be for the population as a whole to have nothing to do with a foreign administration. Those who support such resistance suggest that in the complex world in which we live the total withdrawal of cooperation by the population through strikes, sit-ins, demonstrations and non-participation with the authorities in any way, would make the task of governing a country like Britain impossible.

A central question to ask is whether Britain is more or less secure by virtue of being a member of NATO. Certainly, Britain could not avoid the consequences of any nuclear war fought in Europe, even if it did not participate in the conflict. The effects of nuclear weapons do not respect state boundaries. And NATO would be seriously weakened by a decision by one of its leading and most powerful members to withdraw. Even if the alliance survived, its ability to go on defending its territory and to reinforce the continent would obviously be greatly reduced with all of the dangers of a growing imbalance of military power in Europe. Regardless of Britain's status in any future conflict, its close cultural, economic and political ties with Western Europe and advanced industrial base would make it a major prize for the Soviet Union. The notion that Britain can simply opt out would seem to be a myth.

If, in these circumstances, Britain did find itself involved in a conflict, how effective would the various alternative defence policies be? The answer is that without the support of our allies, particularly the United States, the defence of British territory against an opponent like the Soviet Union would be almost impossible. Britain would be vulnerable to nuclear blackmail and vastly superior military power against which any conventional response would almost certainly fail. Nor would the prospects of civilian or passive resistance be much brighter, even if such resistance could be organised with the support of large sections of the population (which is doubtful). As the Soviet Union has shown in Eastern Europe, if the prize is high enough, overwhelming military power used in a determined way is likely to succeed.

It might be suggested that, even if ultimately these policies did prove ineffective, occupation is preferable to nuclear destruction. This 'red rather than dead' argument has some appeal. If that is the choice, then many people probably would prefer to live under Soviet or any other authoritarian rule. The purpose of any defence policy, however, is to prevent the state having to make that kind of stark choice. If the country's defence policy is ineffective, as most of those discussed above seem to be, the chance of having to confront such a narrow range of options becomes highly likely. If principles or a way of life are worth fighting for, the central objective of any defence policy must be to provide the most credible military posture possible within the limits set by the national economy.

All of the alternatives so far discussed seem to us to have very serious imperfections. Indeed the dangers would appear to be much greater than those created by Britain's contemporary membership of NATO and reliance on a nuclear strategy. This is not, however, the end of the story. It is still possible to ask if there are any other alternative policies which Britain might pursue which avoid the weaknesses and dangers of the present strategy.

HOW MIGHT BRITISH AND NATO STRATEGY BE MODIFIED?

One option not discussed is for Britain to give up its strategic nuclear force but continue to participate fully in a modified NATO nuclear strategy. According to those who argue along these lines, like Lord Carver, Britain's independent deterrent is both dangerous and ineffective. It should therefore be abandoned on practical rather than moral grounds and greater reliance should be placed on the American nuclear umbrella. In its place Britain should improve its conventional contribution to the alliance and try to persuade its allies to do the same in order to raise the nuclear threshold. Unfortunate as it may be, the alliance can never give up reliance on nuclear weapons completely while the Soviet Union continues to possess such weapons. Deterrence must still be maintained at the conventional, theatre nuclear and strategic nuclear levels. Britain would continue to participate in the first two of these levels in order to ensure that the alliance maintains the most effective defence posture it can. This would also require the maintenance of American nuclear bases in Britain, including the proposed cruise missile deployment after 1983, if it becomes necessary.

A variant of this alternative defence option would be for the alliance to place rather less stress on nuclear weapons not only by increasing conventional force levels but also by giving up reliance on short-range tactical (or battlefield) nuclear weapons. The reason for this, it is argued, is that it is difficult to see how such weapons could be used in actual conflict. In general they are stationed close to the front line in Europe and would very likely either be overrun in the early stages of a conflict or be used in a precipitate way. Critics point out that, quite apart from the escalation dangers of such an early release, their short range makes it very difficult to imagine that such weapons could be militarily effective in the fluid environment of war in central Europe.

The inherent dangers of such weapons suggest to many strategic commentators (including the present authors) a strong case for phasing them out. In their place greater reliance could be placed on longer-range theatre nuclear weapons (LRTNF) which would maintain a more effective, less unstable, deterrent at this particular level. Hence the case for the deployment of cruise missiles in Britain. These forces would be situated outside the immediate battle zone giving the opportunity to maintain an extended conventional phase in any conflict and to hit battlefield targets if that was required as a retaliatory strike at a later time. The phasing out of the shorter-range weapons could also leave the nuclear-designated artillery and aircraft on the continent free to concentrate on purely conventional roles.

Such an alternative strategy for Britain and for the alliance, attractive as it seems, is not without its own problems. The reliance on nuclear weapons remains, with all of the dangers if deterrence should break down. In any conflict, and certainly one in which nuclear weapons were used, Britain almost certainly would be subjected to nuclear attack. That possibility, however, has to be weighed against the attempt to enhance deterrence, make it more stable, and erode the dangers of present policy. The greater stress on conventional forces and the ability, if need be, to fight a prolonged conventional war would mean that the Soviet Union in all probability would have to take the very difficult decision of resorting to nuclear weapons first. The greater credibility of a western response, while preserving the options to escalate at the theatre and strategic nuclear levels, would enhance deterrence and thereby make the prospects of any nuclear war in Europe that much less likely.

There are clearly some important advantages therefore in such a modification of alliance strategy and we strongly believe that a move towards a greater emphasis on conventional deterrence should take place. For Britain, however, there is *still* the question of whether strategic nuclear forces ought to be abandoned. Certainly by simply abandoning Polaris or Trident, Britain would not by itself be able to improve the alliance's conventional forces on the scale required for such a modification of alliance strategy. There is also the strong argument that if Britain is to threaten to use theatre nuclear weapons in any conflict, even at a later stage, that threat would not be very credible in deterrent terms unless it was backed up by the threat to use strategic nuclear weapons as well. The threat to use theatre nuclear weapons, without a strategic force to back them up, against an opponent who had both, would not be very convincing. We must now therefore return to the original question: should Britain possess a strategic nuclear deterrent?

SUMMARY OF THE ARGUMENTS

We have looked at the various issues involved in coming to a decision about whether Britain should retain a strategic nuclear capability. We have suggested that, if one believes that there can be no moral justification for a strategy of nuclear deterrence, that such a strategy lessens rather than increases British security, that modernising nuclear systems is beyond Britain's economic resources, or that nuclear weapons have little political utility (or some combination of these judgements), then one's likely conclusion is that Britain should renounce its independent strategic force. However, it has been argued here that neither the moral nor the economic arguments are decisive. Nor do the political arguments seem particularly convincing one way or the other. Some of the strategic arguments, however, do appear to us to have some merit. As a last-resort weapon against nuclear blackmail or a threatened attack on Britain, a nuclear capability would seem to be the most likely way that Britain could retain its independence and integrity through a policy of deterrence. Similarly it seems very difficult to dismiss completely the utility of nuclear weapons in a world in which nuclear proliferation is likely to continue. There is also a case for the possession of a strategic nuclear force by a European state within the NATO alliance.

Even if there is to be a significant change in NATO strategy of the kind we urge – away from short-range nuclear forces to greater stress on conventional forces – there will be a continuing need for long-range theatre nuclear forces and strategic nuclear forces. In both alliance and national terms, British conventional (and theatre nuclear forces) would seem to require a strategic capability to back them up, thereby enhancing the British and NATO deterrent strategies. Such a strategy clearly involves dangers and dilemmas which must be confronted honestly. Nevertheless, nuclear weapons do exist; they cannot be wished away. Marginal as the decision is, it would seem very difficult for politicians, ultimately responsible for the security of the nation, to decide to opt out in such an unstable and unpredictable world. Therefore it does seem to us that the arguments in favour of a British strategic nuclear force are, on balance, stronger than those against. This judgement does not, however, resolve the question of whether the Trident replacement for the present Polaris force is the best option available. It is to that question that we now turn.

IS TRIDENT THE ONLY OR THE BEST OPTION?

In a speech in the House of Commons on 12 March 1982, the Defence Secretary, John Nott, stated that the government remained convinced that 'no other choice but Trident will provide a credible nuclear deterrent into the year 2000 and beyond'. This conclusion resulted, so the 1981 Statement on Defence Estimates confirmed, from a thorough analysis of all of the options available.

The studies which led up to the Government's decision considered various possible launch platforms: sea-based (surface ships or submarines), airborne and land-based . . . Briefly the choice to continue with nuclear-propelled, ocean-going submarines was dictated essentially by the need for invulnerability; other platforms would need to be deployed in large numbers and different operational patterns to give high assurance of surviving sudden attack. The decision of delivery vehicle lay between cruise and ballistic missiles. The former at present cost less each, but much larger numbers are needed for a given level of deterrent threat; and the long-term development of Soviet defences against them is very hard to predict. In addition a cruise missile would need more submarines . . . In short, a cruise missile force would be less certain and more costly than a ballistic missile force.[4]

The government's justification for a submarine-based deterrent would seem to us to be correct. Apart from the essential need for invulnerability, there is also the political and strategic requirement to station nuclear weapons out of sight under the sea rather than base them in Britain itself. The government's argument on cruise missiles is more debatable. The government talks about 'a given level of deterrent threat'. It may well be (indeed it probably is) the case that Britain does not require the same level of deterrent threat as that provided by Trident II (the government was after all perfectly happy with Trident I). If Britain could deter the Soviet Union with less, then there might be a case for a relatively small cruise missile force consisting of ten to twelve nuclear-powered submarines (with twenty or so cruise missiles each). Those submarines might also be dual-capable. That is to say, they might have hunter-killer functions as well as providing the strategic nuclear deterrent.

However, apart from the problems of dual-capable systems (once a submarine fires a missile it immediately becomes vulnerable to detection) there are other difficulties with cruise missiles, as the government statement points out. Each cruise missile has only one warhead; at present they are slow and vulnerable to destruction by Soviet defences; and they also pose inspection problems for arms control negotiations. For these reasons, it does seem that ballistic missiles are preferable as the main component of a strategic deterrent system.

When it comes to choosing between ballistic missiles, the defence white paper argues that, on both cost and operational grounds, Trident has clear advantages. The benefits of Trident (initially the C4 missiles and then the D5 missiles after the October 1981 US decision to accelerate its deployment), are seen to derive from the commonality of cooperation with the United States. It is argued that Britain will benefit (in terms of spare parts, technical information, training assistance and range facilities) from possessing a weapon which remains in service with the US Navy when Britain's own force becomes operational in the 1990s and beyond. Nor is the cost of the force too exhorbitant given the preferential terms offered by the American government.

However, once again the question arises, whether Britain requires the degree of sophistication in terms of the range and accuracy of the missiles which Trident II possesses. The British government argues that such attributes are useful in case of possible anti-ballistic missile (ABM) and anti-submarine warfare (ASW) advances by the Soviet Union towards the end of the century. To have such capabilities, it is stressed, does not involve a change of strategic doctrine (in favour of greater counterforce offensive options). The purpose remains the same; an ability to hit Moscow in a retaliatory strike. The extra sophistication merely provides a cushion or insurance against Soviet technological improvements.

If it is true, however, that Britain *could* make do with less (and in 'selling' Trident the government has never confronted this issue in public), the question is what alternative ballistic missile system might be adopted? There are a number of options worth considering.

First, Britain might continue the Polaris system, which has recently been re-motored and improved with the new Chevaline warhead. Those who support this solution argue that the major problem with the present force is that the submarines will wear out in the 1990s after twenty-five to thirty years in service. The Polaris/Chevaline system, however, is perfectly capable of performing its tasks beyond this date (given the absence of any technological breakthroughs on the horizon). The answer might be to build four or five new submarines and continue with the tried and tested Polaris system. Although the submarines are the costliest component, such a force would be considerably cheaper than Trident (perhaps half the cost).

There is clearly something to be said for such a solution but it does have a number of drawbacks. Apart from not knowing what the state of ABM or ASW technology will be in the year 2000, there is also the difficulty of maintaining an ageing missile in service when American facilities and production lines have long been closed down. Such support might be bought but the cost would be high and the chances of major failures in the system as it got older would be greater. Given the need for a high level of reliability, such an option is clearly not as attractive as it first appears. If the new submarines were given enlarged missile tubes however, which would be relatively easy to do, such an arrangement might conceivably be used as an interim measure until a new missile was bought or developed.

Another possible option is for Britain, largely for Gaullist reasons, to try to go it alone. Some believe that dependence in such a vital field on the Americans in perpetuity is not a sound policy. Efforts should therefore be made to get back into the missile production business and develop a purely British system. There is little doubt that Britain could do this if it so wished. The problem clearly is one of cost. To create the infrastructure needed to reestablish ballistic missile development would be very expensive indeed and the cost would be considerably more than the present figure of £7500 million to be spent on Trident. The £1000 million spent on the British Chevaline project indicates the financial difficulties of such an option. The French experience should also be borne in mind. The attempt to maintain a wholly independent system has been achieved but over the years France's conventional forces have suffered as a result. If Britain wishes to improve its conventional forces this would seem to be a difficult option to choose unless defence spending were significantly increased: a prospect which would be politically difficult to achieve.

Another option, touched upon earlier, is that of Anglo-French cooperation. As we suggested there clearly are difficulties in such cooperation. They may not, however, be insuperable in the longer term. Cooperation could conceivably take a number of forms: pooling resources to produce an Anglo-French force; purchasing the French M4 missile; or collaborating in the deployment of existing forces (as a basis for future technological cooperation).

The most difficult of the three would involve the production of a joint force. In many ways it would be logical for Britain to contribute warhead technology and France missile technology to an Anglo-French venture. Both are after all medium powers with similar problems and collaboration in other fields has proved reasonably successful. As we suggested earlier, however, French stress on independence and the restrictions on Britain passing on US information make this very difficult, at least at present.

The purchase of the M4 missile rather than Trident would have the advantage of emphasising Britain's European links and providing the UK with a missile more suited to its needs. Britain would, however, almost certainly have to pay quite a high price for the M4 (without the preferential fixed research and development payment offered for Trident). Although it is a fairly new missile (now), it is little better than Polaris. Furthermore such a purchase would be likely to cut Britain off from the wide range of ancillary cooperation with the United States (particularly in terms of satellite intelligence, communications and navigational facilities). Some cooperation in these fields might occur with France but Britain clearly benefits far more from its nuclear partnership with the US.

There are perhaps some opportunities to initiate a more limited form of Anglo-French cooperation by greater collaboration in the deployment of the strategic forces of both countries. Britain usually has one boat on station at any time (although sometimes two) and France usually has two or three. Some agreement might be achieved to make sure that there were always four boats at sea forming a much more formidable combined deterrent to any aggressor than the separate forces of both countries. Once again, however, despite the apparent attractiveness of such cooperation, the obstacle of national independence (for Britain as much as for France) is a difficult one to overcome. Such joint deployment would involve mutual dependence in a vital area of security policy and would also probably imply some joint targeting arrangements.

The political difficulties of any of these forms of Anglo-French cooperation therefore remain. There is a case, however, for at least considering this option in some depth. Given the economic pressures of maintaining viable deterrent forces, the political advantages of greater European cooperation and the complementary nature of the forces of both countries, the possibilities of overcoming the political problems in the longer term should not be ignored. Indeed it might be possible for Britain to persuade the United States to relax the regulations on the transfer of information to third parties and to assist both Britain and France. For the United States the goal of greater European collaboration might make this worthwhile. For France, similarly, such collaboration might lessen the economic strain and pull Britain more effectively into the future development of Europe. The difficulties cannot be ignored, yet these are options for the 1990s and beyond which might be looked at in more depth than it seems they have been in recent years.

What conclusions does this discussion suggest? Despite the criticisms of Trident, if Britain does require a strategic nuclear capability this looks like the most cost-effective option. Trident II's capabilities are, however, more sophisticated than Britain requires; it is costly and may well have an adverse effect on Britain's conventional capability in the future; and it does maintain Britain's strategic dependence on the United States. For these reasons it would seem logical for Britain to search for a cheaper option which does not necessarily have the same deterrent power. It is surely not necessary, for example, for Britain to be able to destroy Moscow if it can hit other major Soviet cities. Although the next generation of cruise missiles should not be totally dismissed, it would seem preferable to go for a submarine-based ballistic missile. This seems to us to point to a stop-gap measure which involves continuing Polaris/Chevaline for as long as possible (and perhaps even putting them into new and bigger submarines) until future technological and political developments become clearer. In the longer term it may be possible to achieve some kind of collaboration with Britain's European partners (perhaps in the form of Anglo-French or American–British–French cooperation). The important point is that the decision about the future of the British nuclear deterrent must be set in the wider context of NATO strategy and Britain's relations with its allies. If NATO can be persuaded to support a strategic shift in favour of conventional forces, Britain should play its part in this process. This does not mean relinquishing some form of nuclear capability but it does suggest a relative switch of priorities away from the most expensive and sophisticated nuclear systems towards a greater conventional contribution to alliance defence. If this movement towards conventional deterrence takes place, Britain would still require some kind of nuclear capability as an insurance against unforeseen contingencies. The point being made here, however, is that a change of NATO strategy would, in itself, enhance British security and as such Britain would not require a nuclear capability with the kind of exacting standards of deterrence which are characteristic of the Trident system.

It could be, of course, that after detailed studies the alternatives suggested above prove impossible to achieve. Equally it may not be possible to persuade Britain's allies to move as far as Britain would like in the desired direction of improving alliance conventional forces. In such circumstances Trident might still be taken up at a later date. For the moment, however, a much more positive approach to finding an alternative which is cheaper (allowing Britain to improve its conventional forces) and which involves some form of European cooperation (preferably supported by the United States) we feel should be earnestly undertaken.

REFERENCES

1. L. Freedman, *Britain and Nuclear Weapons* (Macmillan, 1980) p. 129.
2. *Second Report from the Expenditure Committee*, session 1975–6 (SCOE 73/1).
3. H. Bull, 'Future Conditions of Strategic Deterrence', in C. Bertram (ed.), *The Future of Strategic Deterrence* (Macmillan, 1981) p. 16.
4. *Statement on the Defence Estimates 1981*, Cmnd. 8212–1, pp. 12, 14.

Conclusion

GERALD SEGAL, EDWINA MORETON, LAWRENCE FREEDMAN, JOHN BAYLIS

There is no simple way to untie the nuclear knot. This creates complex and perplexing problems. To recognise it does not imply a complacent or uncaring attitude towards the dangers of nuclear war. If anything it increases the agony. It is precisely because of these dangers that it is necessary to apply so much thought and energy to controlling the most dangerous aspects of the nuclear balance and the most turbulent features of international relations.

Control and reduction rather than elimination of nuclear weapons has been a theme of this book. There are no utopian solutions to the threat of nuclear war for two basic reasons. Once nuclear weapons were invented, they could not be uninvented. Nuclear knowledge has spread around the globe. Even if it were possible for today's nuclear states to agree to eliminate all their nuclear weapons, the diffusion of nuclear knowledge and the threat that such knowledge could be used by the unscrupulous make it fruitless to turn back the clock.

Moreover, the weapons themselves are tools in a political process. The dangers of nuclear weapons, as with other weapons, stem from their use by politicians in pursuit of political ends. Conflict will remain a basic feature of international politics, whether it be Nazi Germany versus the Allies, Israel versus the Arabs, or the Soviet Union versus the United States.

This pessimism about utopian visions is not to suggest that there is nothing that can be done. Certainly, some are under the illusion that everything can be done, while others have the illusion that there is no alternative but to despair. Both sentiments are misplaced. It has been possible to live since 1945 with the dangers of nuclear weapons, without those weapons being used in international conflict. It has

153

even been possible to turn the threat to advantage by using it to warn the major powers off war.

The contemporary conflict in which nuclear weapons figure so prominently is the one between east and west – between the United States and the Soviet Union. One does not need to exaggerate the conflict to recognise that it is real and based on more than a misperception of each other's armaments. Mutual suspicions and conflicting interests make it impossible for either side to trust the other. The Soviet Union is an adversary power against which it is only prudent to plan to defend.

This defence must include nuclear weapons because the Soviet Union also has such weapons. It must also include sufficient conventional forces to reduce reliance on nuclear weapons. But prudent defence need not and should not mean open-ended military spending. For some, preoccupied with dark threats and incapable of keeping Soviet power in perspective, there can never be enough. Given the extent to which deterrence seems to have worked up until now, the pedlars of gloom among the hawks should be surprised that somehow their most dire predictions have not come to pass. The west must search for a minimum deterrent. We only ask that the 'minimum' refers to risks as well as costs and weapons numbers.

Deterrence of nuclear war still rests on the mutual threat of assured destruction. This deterrence is not nearly as fragile as many critics suggest. Nevertheless, even if it is more robust than many think, there are many complicating and dangerous aspects of this balance that can be greatly reduced.

This task offers real and vital opportunities for arms control. By limiting the most dangerous weapons, the risks of war by miscalculation can be reduced. The aim must be to reduce the nuclear stockpile to the minimum necessary for a secure second strike. Thus deep cuts can be made in other, more dangerous categories of weapons. For example, the particularly destabilising category of land-based ICBMs could be sharply cut. Battlefield nuclear weapons in Europe can go the same way. There is no harm for the sake of a strategy that is both more coherent and comforting to the people it is designed to protect, to consider taking unilateral steps to eliminate these types of systems. It would be best if this could be achieved in arms control negotiations, because the move is less revocable and clearly reciprocated.

Arms control has lately received a bad press. Yet it still offers a realistic path to reducing the dangers of nuclear war and has already more to its credit than is commonly realised. The roomy walls and high ceilings of earlier arms control agreements can now be reduced in size. But talks will not be easy. The superpowers are not aiming to do each other a favour by negotiating arms control. Their purpose is to secure their own defence and enhance their own security. Arms control will work best if it can offer the hope of doing both at lower cost and lower risk.

The one place where the superpower confrontation appears most acute is in Europe, where forces of east and west are deployed in greatest numbers. In this arena, as in the strategic nuclear balance, the risks of nuclear war and the excessive number of weapons can be significantly reduced. Some of those weapons are more destabilising than others. Battlefield nuclear weapons, including the neutron warhead, are particularly dangerous. Others, despite their adverse publicity, can be used to reinforce the more sensible features of current NATO doctrine. It may well be necessary to deploy new intermediate-range weapons – cruise and Pershing missiles – on the western side if current negotiations fail to produce results. The present debate over these missiles is only part of a long-standing debate over how to couple the commitment of United States power to the defence of Western Europe. There are no simple solutions to this coupling problem, which is a creation of geography as much as anything else. One large step forward would be for NATO to strengthen conventional deterrence. This would reduce the burden on the United States of having to provide incredible and distasteful threats of nuclear first use in order to make up for deficiencies in conventional forces that the Europeans have allowed to develop. If the nuclear threshold can be raised, the dangers of nuclear war in Europe will be correspondingly reduced.

Such a move would require greater Western European defence cooperation. If this could be achieved, then we might also find the key to the particular problem of Britain's own nuclear weapons. Britain's strategic needs are very much bound up with those of its allies and should be viewed accordingly. There is no need to be dogmatic about the type of weapons best suited to Britain if some are deemed necessary. It is necessary to negotiate about the reduction or elimination of weapons while simultaneously preparing for Europe's own defence. Western Europe is best served by NATO backed up by the US guarantee, but there is still a need for an independent voice in defence and the retention of some capability just in case the US umbrella is ever removed.

We live in a nuclear age, and in all probability it will remain the nuclear age for many decades. This is a disturbing prospect but one that does not inevitably involve disaster. Our prescription is threefold. First, nobody is served by wishful thinking or a false prospectus. The result of a failure to achieve the impossible is likely to be disillusionment or despair. The nuclear issue is too important for the occasional burst of campaigning to be followed by weary apathy. It requires continual attention. Second, there is much that can be done through the time-consuming and intricate mechanisms of arms control to ease the strains of the nuclear age. We can at least ensure that nuclear weapons are not allowed to drive diplomacy or intrude too easily into crises. Third, and probably most important, we must never forget that the sources of war are to be found in political relations and not in some mechanical outcome of an arms race. In the end there is no substitute for old-fashioned statescraft calming the impulses to war. As much patience and intricate handiwork must go into loosening the nuclear knot, as was used in its original weaving.

Select Bibliography

General reading on nuclear weapons is often hard to find because of extreme views or technical obfuscation. Three books do attempt a balanced approach: L. Freedman, *The Evolution of Nuclear Strategy* (Macmillan, 1981); J. Baylis, K. Booth, J. Garnett and P. Williams, *Contemporary Strategy* (Croom Helm, 1975); and D. Snow, *Nuclear Strategy in a Dynamic World* (University of Alabama, 1981). A few other books are either somewhat dated, or deal with limited aspects of the broad subject of strategy but are still very useful: B. Brodie, *Strategy in the Missile Age* (Princeton University Press, 1959); R. Jervis, *Perception and Misperception in International Politics* (Princeton University Press, 1976); and T. Schelling, *Arms and Influence* (Yale University Press, 1966). Most data on weapons are based on the annual volumes of the *Military Balance* (International Institute for Strategic Studies). The proliferation of articles on the subject makes it pointless to list them, but some of the more thoughtful contemporary debates are carried on in the pages of *International Security* and *Foreign Policy*.

The mass of paperbacks on nuclear weapons subjects seems at times to keep the pulp business going. The more notable books on the left include J. Cox, *Overkill* (Penguin, 1981); J. McMahan, *British Nuclear Weapons: For and Against* (Junction Books, 1981); R. Nield, *How to Make Up Your Mind about the Bomb* (Deutsch, 1981); P. Rogers, M. Dando and P. Van Den Dungen, *As Lambs to the Slaughter* (Arrow Books, 1981); and E. P. Thompson and D. Smith (eds), *Protest and Survive* (Penguin, 1980). See also the related book by M. Kaldor, *The Baroque Arsenal* (Deutsch, 1982). Other interesting books on this subject but with less radical views are S. Zuckerman, *Nuclear Illusion and Reality* (Collins, 1982); N. Calder, *Nuclear Nightmares* (Penguin, 1981); L. Martin, *The Two-edged Sword* (Weidenfeld and Nicolson, 1982); and E. Kennedy and M. Hatfield, *Freeze* (Bantam, 1982).

Of the vast literature on more specific problems of strategy, some of the better books are K. Booth, *Strategy and Ethnocentrism* (Croom Helm, 1979); M. Mandelbaum, *The Nuclear Revolution* (Cambridge University Press, 1981); D. Ball, 'Can Nuclear War Be Controlled', *Adelphi Papers*, no. 169, Autumn 1981; see also the *Adelphi Papers*, nos. 160, 161, 165 for current discussions of deterrence and arms control; also, L. Martin (ed.), *Strategic Thought in the Nuclear Age* (Heinemann, 1979); C. Gray, *The Soviet–American Arms Race* (Saxon House, 1976); A. George and R. Smoke, *Deterrence in American Foreign Policy* (Columbia University Press, 1974); and P. Williams, *Crisis Management* (Martin Robertson, 1976).

On issues of morality, apart from parts of books already cited, see G. Goodwin (ed.), *Ethics and Nuclear Deterrence* (Croom Helm, 1982). On the impact of nuclear weapons and its probable destruction see United States Congress, Office of Technology Assessment, *The Effects of Nuclear War* (USGPO, 1979); and P. Godwin, *Nuclear War: The Facts* (Macmillan, 1982).

The literature on the Soviet Union is too vast to list here. A summary and centre ground is provided in J. Baylis and G. Segal (eds), *Soviet Strategy* (Croom Helm, 1981). See also the superb study by S. Kaplan, *Diplomacy of Power* (Brookings, 1981) and a useful pamphlet by F. Kaplan, *Dubious Spectre* (Institute for Policy Studies, Washington, 1980).

For additionally useful material but of a more conservative nature see D. Leebaert, *Soviet Military Thinking* (George Allen and Unwin, 1981); E. Warner, *The Military in Contemporary Soviet Politics* (Praeger, 1977); T. Wolfe, *Soviet Power and Europe 1945–70* (Johns Hopkins University Press, 1970); and H. F. Scott and W. F. Scott, *The Armed Forces of the USSR* (Westview, 1979). On civil defence see F. Kaplan, 'The Soviet Civil Defence Myth', *The Bulletin of the Atomic Scientists*, vol. 34, nos 3 and 4, March and April 1978.

On proliferation see two provocative works, one by K. Waltz, 'The Spread of Nuclear Weapons: More May be Better', *Adelphi Papers*, no. 171, Autumn 1981, and the other by E. Lefever, *Nuclear Arms in the Third World* (Brookings, 1979). See also L. Dunn, *Controlling the Bomb* (Yale University Press, 1982).

On arms control, apart from some of the general books cited, see also J. Newhouse, *Cold Dawn* (Holt, Rinehart and Winston, 1973); and S. Talbott, *Endgame* (Harper and Row, 1979). More academic, but useful studies include T. Wolfe, *The SALT Experience* (Ballinger, 1979); M. Willrich and J. Rhinelander, *SALT* (The Free Press, 1974); W. Panofsky, *Arms Control and SALT II* (University of Washington Press, 1979); and C. Bertram (ed.), *Arms Control and Military Force* (Gower, 1980).

For some reading specifically on European issues see two challenging books on the left by E. P. Thompson, *Zero Option* (Merlin, 1982) and M. Kaldor and D. Smith (eds), *Disarming Europe* (Merlin, 1982). Less outspoken writing on the subject includes A. Grosser, *The Western Alliance* (Macmillan, 1981); J. I. Coffey, *Arms Control and European Security* (Chatto and Windus, 1977; now published by Macmillan); L. Hagen (ed.), *The Crisis in Western Security* (Croom Helm, 1982); W. Gutteridge (ed.), *European Security, Nuclear Weapons and Public Confidence* (Macmillan, 1982); C. Bell, *European Security* (Heath, 1979); H. J. Neuman, *Nuclear Forces in Europe* (IISS, 1982); and L. Freedman, *Arms Control in Europe* (Chatham House Papers no. 11, 1981).

The literature on Britain and the bomb includes numerous books on the left cited in the second paragraph. See also D. Smith, *The Defence of the Realm in the 1980s* (Croom Helm, 1980) and M. Kaldor, D. Smith and S. Vines (eds), *Domestic Socialism and the Cost of Defence* (Croom Helm, 1979). For relevant academic works see A. Pierre, *Nuclear Politics* (Oxford University Press, 1972); M. Gowing, *Independence and Deterrence* (Macmillan, 1974); J. Baylis, *British Defence Policy in a Changing World* (Croom Helm, 1977); and J. Baylis, *Anglo-American Defence Relations* (Macmillan, 1981). See also L. Freedman, *Britain and Nuclear Weapons* (Macmillan, 1980).

Index

ABM (anti-ballistic missiles), 62,
148, 149
ABM treaty, 43–5, 53, 72, 73, 75
Action–reaction pattern, 21
Afghanistan, 10, 34, 35, 37, 47, 99,
118, 136
Africa, 11
Agreement on Measures to Reduce
the Risks of Outbreak of
Nuclear War (accidents
agreement), 73
Agreement on the Prevention of
Incidents On and Over the High
Sea, 73
Albania, 10
ALCM (air-launched cruise
missiles), 46
Alliances, 110–13
Anglo-French cooperation, 150
Anti-nuclear movement, 34, 39, 113
Anti-satellite weapons (ASAT),
70–3
Anti-submarine warfare, 69, 148,
149
Argentina, 129, 130
Arms control, 18, 23, 34, 106–10,
147
  building confidence in, 73–4
  critical choices for, 63–5
  cuts in number of nuclear
      weapons, 57–9
  defence of, 40–53
  failure of, 110
  flaws in, 54
  future of 74–7
  guidelines for, 106–7
  opportunities for, 154–5
  philosophy of, 39
  problems facing, 76

progress in, 77
underlying principles of, 74–6
Arms control agreement, 18, 40–1,
65
Arms race, 20–6, 137
Arms spending, 18, 28, 104–5,
133–5, 137
ASBM (air-to-surface ballistic
missile), 46
Assured destruction doctrine, 15
Atomic bomb, 1, 18, 83, 90
Atomic weapons, 10, 13
Austria, 10, 11

Balance of power, 7
Baltic states, 9, 10
Berlin crises, 28
Biological warfare, 4, 19
Brazil, 138
Brezhnev, President, 44
Britain, 10, 116–52
British Army of the Rhine (BAOR),
140
Bull, Hedley, 131

C4 missiles, 148
Campaign for Nuclear Disarmament
(CND), 116, 135, 139, 142
  objectives, 137–8
  popularity of, 138
  resurgence of, 136
Canada, 141
Capitalism, 8
Carter, President, 46, 51, 59, 67, 97
Carver, Lord, 125, 126, 144
Chemical weapons, 4, 19
Chevaline warhead, 148, 151
China, 9, 10, 30, 31
Civil defence, 29–31

159